CLOSE ENCOUNTERS WITH ACCOUNTABILITY CITIZENSHIP

Critical Thinking on American Politics and Government

STEPHEN TRYON

AccountabilityCitizenship.org

CLOSE ENCOUNTERS WITH ACCOUNTABILITY CITIZENSHIP

Publisher's Cataloging-In-Publication Data
(Prepared by The Donohue Group, Inc.)

Names: Tryon, Stephen, author.
Title: Close encounters with accountability citizenship : critical
    thinking on American politics and government / Stephen Tryon.
Description: [Salt Lake City, Utah] : AccountabilityCitizenship.org,
    [2021] | Include bibliographical references.
Identifiers: ISBN 9781734304701 (paperback) | ISBN 9781734304718 (ePub)
Subjects: LCSH: United States--Politics and government--Philosophy. |
    Critical thinking. | Reasoning. | Public policy. | Social problems--
    United States--21st century.
Classification: LCC JK31 .T79 2021 (print) | LCC JK31 (ebook) | DDC
    320.973--dc23

First Printing, 2021

Cover Design by AccountabilityCitizenship.org. Front cover art "Close Encounters With Accountability", Cover art and photo by Stephen Tryon.

"Facts are stubborn things; and whatever may be our wishes, our inclinations, or the dictates of our passion, they cannot alter the state of facts and evidence."
John Adams, 2d President of the United States

"And when you trust your television
What you get is what you got
'Cause when they own the information, oh
They can bend it all they want."
John Mayer "Waiting on the World to Change"

For my sister and all my brothers, the best role models anyone could have.

CONTENTS

PREFACE

The purpose of this book is to help readers understand how to sort and evaluate information about public policy and matters of governance in the United States. We are all confronted with a lot of information every day. To survive, we sort that information into facts, evidence, hypotheses, conclusions and opinions. We evaluate hypotheses, conclusions and opinions based on how we believe the facts and evidence support them.

But we do not all understand how human brains and bodies limit our ability to consistently and accurately complete this process of evaluation. And we do not all apply the same skills and definitions to the process of evaluation. As a result, many are making evaluations and choosing elected officials based on a set of "facts" that are not really facts at all. The disparity in understanding the limits we all share and the wide divergence in what is considered to be fact contributes to conflict and division in our society.

We can reduce the conflict and division if we increase the general level of understanding of the issues discussed in this book. Sections I and VI are introduction and conclusion. Sections II through V present a series of essays on issues of governance, cognitive bias and the historical standards we have used to determine whether something is true or false. Each section ends with a set of key terms and study questions. Appendix 1 is an overview of critical reasoning, and Appendix 2 provides possible solutions to the study questions. Throughout, you will find readings on American politics and government paired with material that will illuminate the reasoning used to support conclusions.

It is certainly possible to read each section in order. Each chapter is an essay. With the exception of Chapter 1, each is taken from my blog at accountabilitycitizenship.org. The original date of publication is provided for reference, but I have organized the essays to support the purpose of this book rather than chronologically. Teachers may find it helpful to assign readings from Appendix 1 or the chapters on bias and truth in the same lesson block with an essay on a challenge or recommendation. Either approach affords the reader an opportunity to analyze arguments in the readings as well as to support arguments of their own.

PART I

Overture

Bottom Line Up Front

The main idea of this book is that the principal virtues of the American Republic should be humility, tolerance in pursuit of truth, and compromise. Chapter 1 describes how this thesis emerged. We are trying to solve big problems. We have trouble sorting through a flood of information. Some people stop thinking, hiding inside a religion, a political affiliation, or with like-minded friends. Others struggle to find answers alone. The main idea of this book is that none of us get to the right answer without thinking for ourselves and sharing our reasoning with others. That is what it means to be a social animal--we need each other to eliminate our collective blind spots. Chapter 2 was one of the first blogs: I knew I had to start the journey, but did not know where it would lead. It has brought me to suggest a set of values (humility, tolerance, compromise) and a set of tools (technologies, procedures, and laws). This book is not the end of the journey, but it may help us start to walk together again.

CHAPTER 1

Introduction

The master virtues of our republic should be humility, tolerance and compromise. That's what I want you to remember from this book.

I did not start out with that thesis. In fact, I didn't start out with any thesis. I was writing blog posts for my web site, accountabilitycitizenship.org. I wrote about the space where current events intersected with the topic of the book Accountability Citizenship—about getting citizens engaged and informed enough to vote in support of values aligned with our Constitution.

I believed at the outset that much of the polarization we experience in our public space comes from people who are uninformed, or misinformed, about our Constitution. The argument was that the Constitution embodied a set of mutually consistent principles, that we as Americans accepted the Constitution as a contract amongst ourselves, and that we should therefore be able to reduce polarization and even generate consensus by increasing understanding of the Constitution.

I still believe this is part of the truth, but there's a "catch."

Constitutional principles can be mutually consistent, but they are not necessarily so. For instance, we can both agree individual liberty is a constitutional principle, but disagree on where to draw the line when it conflicts with another principle like the welfare of the public. People bring their values to the table when they weigh the relative importance of conflicting constitutional principles. Our individual values can vary a great deal. Values may spring from moral and religious beliefs, life experiences, educational background, and other factors.

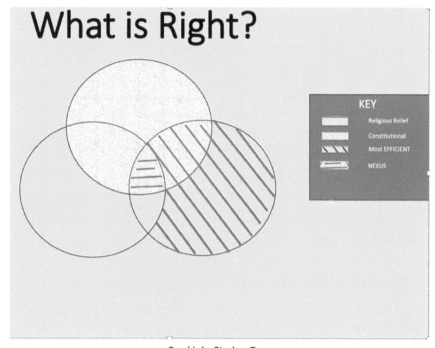

Graphic by Stephen Tryon

We need look no further than the recent controversy over wearing face masks for an example of a conflict of values: some people believe a mandatory face mask requirement is justifiable because it protects the right to life for other members of the community. Others feel the evidence correlating face-mask-wearing with the safety of others is not strong enough, or that it should be the responsibility of vulnerable people to stay away from public spaces rather than imposing a restriction on everyone using those public spaces.

In some cases, constitutional principles do not seem to be consistent at all. The Constitution establishes procedures for resolving the inevitable conflicts between competing interests. Some people do not respect the outcomes of those procedures unless they agree with them, and even seek to bend the procedures themselves in order to get the outcome they want. The fact that the Supreme Court has ruled that abortion is legal under some circumstances (*Roe v. Wade*) has led to almost 50 years of protests from those who believe that abortion is murder—a violation of the right to life. Protesters have gone so far as to murder doctors who perform abortions as a means to protect the right to life they assert for the unborn.

Some people adopt positions that favor individual liberty in some cases while opposing individual liberty in others. Many of those who oppose face mask requirements on the basis of individual liberty, for instance, deny that a woman can exercise individual liberty in choosing to have an abortion at any point in her pregnancy. The opposite contradictory views also occur: people assert the right of a woman to have an abortion based on an argument from individual liberty while supporting mandatory restrictions on individual liberty in the case of motorcycle helmet laws, face mask requirements, and gun control.

Some can articulate the reason why they believe the balance of constitutional principles breaks in different ways on these various issues, but many cannot. Many have not considered the possible conflict between policy positions, while others embrace a religious or political party affiliation that serves as a proxy for their own individual thought process. Regardless of how they have adopted their position, many are simply unwilling or unable to consider the merit of the opposing view in a non-emotional manner.

No one can deny that there is an overwhelming volume of information to support both sides of nearly every controversy such as that arising between abortion and individual liberty. The information is often complex and accompanied with some degree of uncertainty. In order to achieve a nonviolent resolution of these issues, people on both sides must be willing to consider the merits of the opposing arguments. To be capable of such consideration, people must have both access to reliable information and the intellectual capacity to evaluate that information. In thinking and writing about the areas where constitutional principles conflict, I repeatedly found myself confronting the importance of citizens being willing to listen to opposing views as well as the necessity for people to evaluate information consistently.

As I began to consider what I had learned from several years of blogging about these issues, it occurred to me that I might group the essays into four main groups. Those groups then became the major sections of this book. The essays in Chapter 2 (Challenges) discuss areas where value conflicts or systemic constraints hinder the effectiveness of our federal government. The essays in Chapter 3 (Fix Yourself First) encourage people to consider the implications of our social nature as well as the limits of our ability as individuals to fully grasp all sides of social conflicts. The essays in Chapter 4 (Facts & Fake News) describe time-tested methods for consistently evaluating which of two or more competing theories is the most credible. Finally, the essays in Chapter 5 (Changes We Need) offer some thoughts on systemic and individual changes that could help resolve issues and improve the effectiveness of government.

As I stood back from the essays that make up these four chapters, the thesis emerged. What I believe I have learned from eight years of writing about accountability and citizenship is simply this: we need humility, a tolerant pursuit of the truth, and a systemic bias towards compromise if we are to preserve our republic. We must be humble enough to recognize our individual perspectives are probably flawed and incomplete. We must consistently apply the yardsticks of truth and reason to the complex facts supporting competing hypotheses to have a reasonable chance of generating consensus. We must repair systems that have been warped in favor of partisanship so that they facilitate compromise.

The master virtues of our republic should be humility, tolerance in pursuit of the truth and compromise. That's what I want you to remember from this book.

CHAPTER 2

Close Encounters With Accountability Citizenship

"Close Encounters With Accountability"
Painting and Photo by Stephen Tryon

Originally published July 10, 2015.

I remember a movie from the 70's called *Close Encounters of the Third Kind*... it was one of Steven Spielberg's hits and starred Richard Dreyfus and won a bunch of awards. The idea was that this fellow saw a UFO and then had an overwhelming urge to make a big clay mess in his living room for reasons even he could not explain or understand. Well, you can imagine what this kind of behavior does for those around him--they all think he's nuts. Of course, he somehow discovers that the thing he built is a model of Devil's Tower, Wyoming, and he is off on his quest, which leads ultimately to first contact with extraterrestrial aliens. If you haven't seen this movie, it's worth watching.

I've taken to explaining my AccountabilityCitizenship.org quest by relating the story line of *Close Encounters of the Third Kind*. I feel a bit like the Dreyfus character. Writing the book *Accountability Citizenship* and launching this web site and even running for Congress in 2014 and 2016: these are my messy clay models. I was inspired--impelled perhaps-- to these actions by close encounters with accountability over decades of leadership in government and in business.

You see, I have been on teams my whole adult life, and those teams have worked with other teams to solve difficult, complex problems. Every time one of these situations occurred, there are always some on each team who start by finding another team to blame. That never solves anything. And then we have passionate team-solution advocates, who argue incessantly for a course of action that mainly addresses their team's part of the problem. Sprinkle a few of these people on each team, and you get incessant arguing and no solutions.

In fact, the only way my teams have ever made progress solving complex problems was by breaking the problem down to the individual level. What are individuals, whether customers or people trying to serve customers, experiencing? What is it about the individual cases that make this problem large and complex? Building a picture from the grassroots level allows everyone to see more clearly the actions that are necessary to address the many individual experiences of the problem. Clearly, at this point, some prioritization of solutions becomes necessary, but the process of breaking down the problem gives us some objective data--number of customers affected or dollars lost or something--that makes agreeing on priorities easier.

And once specific actions and priorities are on the table, we can talk about who should be accountable for doing them. What needs to be done? Who can do it? How can we make them accountable for doing it? Ultimately, if we hold people accountable for specific actions that solve individual instances of the problem, the complex problem gets smaller. The kernel of every solution to difficult, complex problems starts with identifying solutions to individual instances of the problem, not with advocating one team's philosophical solution and certainly not with blaming others.

My experience with complex problems combined with decades of listening to our national political news impelled me to write *Accountability Citizenship* and create the website AccountabilityCitizenship.org. You cannot listen or read or watch any news these days without being bombarded with all the complex problems we are trying to solve on the national political scene. And we have lots of blamers, and lots of people willing to advocate for their team's optimal solution but darn few people who seem willing to do the hard work that will really generate solutions to those complex problems. And in the last election, most of the registered voters in my state just stayed home and didn't participate. I mean, what's the use, right?

Well, no. That's not right. It's wrong. Because when you break down whatever difficult, complex National Political Problem bothers you the most, one of the actions that is necessary to address your individual experience of that problem is for you to communicate your individual perspective. What we lack at the national level is a clear consensus on anything. What passes for consensus is simply one party-solution advocate's proposal that happens to triumph over another party-solution advocate's proposal in a particular election by a narrow margin of the fifty percent or so of us who care enough to show up. I don't know what all the actions are that will resolve the issues of health care and immigration and how much we should spend on defense or highways or the space program. Even if I did, I do not have the ability to take all those actions. But I know that what is needed for every problem is a real consensus on a solution, and I know that I can take specific actions to help shape that consensus. Voting is one of those actions. Writing letters and emails to appropriate officials is another. In fact, the toolkit I propose in *Accountability Citizenship* is precisely the set of actions I think individuals should take to help resolve the difficult, complex problems of gridlock and ineffective government. That's why I wrote it. That's why I'm breaking it down even more with blogs on a web site called AccountabilityCitizenship.org. These actions are the only part of a solution I can control. So here I am.

Come on in. Visit the web site and register. You might win some cool free stuff. But watch out for the mud in the living room.

Study Questions And Key Terms

STUDY QUESTIONS

1. What are the five most important national political problems facing the United States today?

2. For one of the five problems you identified complete the following analysis: (a) Why is this problem so important? (b) Does the problem involve a conflict of constitutional principles? Which constitutional principles are in conflict? (c) List the values that support each side of the conflict. (d) How do you think the conflict should be resolved?

3. In Essay 1, the author states that he began his blogging project with the belief that that the Constitution was built around mutually consistent principles. Based on this belief, the author thought that increasing understanding of these consistent principles would enable compromise. Using the principles of critical reasoning identified in Appendix 1, one way we might describe the author's original argument is as follows:

> **Premise 1**: If the Constitution consists of mutually consistent principles, then ensuring full understanding of the principles will enable political compromise.
>
> **Premise 2**: The Constitution consists of mutually consistent principles.
>
> **Conclusion**: Ensuring understanding of these principles will enable compromise.

Why does the author now believe his original argument was flawed?

4. In Essay 1, the author concludes that the master virtues of our republic should be humility, tolerance in pursuit of truth, and compromise. What reasons does the author use to support this conclusion? Can you organize the author's thoughts into an argument supporting his conclusion?

1. **value** - an individual's principles, standards of behavior, or judgment of relative importance
2. **Constitution of the United States** – a document that embodies the fundamental laws and principles by which the US is governed
3. **religion** - the belief in and worship of a superhuman controlling power, especially a personal God or gods
4. **moral theory** - an explanation of how we should determine right or wrong conduct; a framework for evaluating moral issues
5. **humility** - the quality of having a modest view of one's own importance
6. **tolerance** - the ability to abide the existence of opinions or behavior with which one does not necessarily agree
7. **truth** - that which is in accordance with facts, reality, or the universe of shared experience as confirmed by correspondence, coherence, and falsifiability/predictability
8. **compromise** - an agreement or settlement reached by each party making concessions
9. **reason** - the power of the mind to think, understand, and form judgments by a process of logic
10. **virtue** - a good and moral quality; the embodiment of one or more of an individual's or group's moral values
11. **political party** - an organized group professing the same political ideology
12. **liberty** - the state of being free from oppressive restrictions on one's way of life, behavior or political views
13. **national political problem** - a conflict between groups over policies, resources and authority that can or does affect the entire country
14. **effectiveness** - the degree to which something is successful in producing a desired result
15. **efficiency** - the state of using the smallest quantity of resources to achieve the best possible outcome

PART II

Challenges

Bottom Line Up Front

This section identifies some of the challenges we need to address to keep the American Dream alive in the 21st century. In this Information Age, we must ensure Americans know how to evaluate information to determine what is true and what is not true (Ch 3). We must understand how our information environment puts us in filter bubbles, and how to escape our bubble (Ch 4). We must constantly seek equality of opportunity for all Americans (Ch 5, 6). To achieve this, we must select the best candidates for public office, and we must carefully monitor and adapt the structures that support our elections and guarantee transparency from the people we elect (Ch 7). Finally, we must get dark money out of our electoral systems and create a level playing field for candidates (Ch 8).

CHAPTER 3

Thoughts on the Eve of the 2018 Election

Originally published November 5, 2018.

Two things I've learned about my fellow Americans during the past three years bother me: (1) Too many of you are unable or unwilling to decide for yourselves what is true and what is false; and (2) Too many of you put loyalty to your political party ahead of loyalty to the principles for which our country is supposed to stand.

When Donald Trump hears something critical of himself or his policies, he declares it is "fake news," *Photo by Stephen Tryon*
and too many of you just swallow his assessment uncritically. You should be able to decide for yourself what is true and what is false. We say that we know something when the statement describing that thing rises to the level of "justified true belief." A statement rises to the level of justified true belief when it corresponds to the world in such a way that it is (a) independently verifiable (or falsifiable), and (b) coherent with a broader set of justified true beliefs.

"Independently verifiable" doesn't mean that your cousin agrees with the statement. It means that the overwhelming majority of credible sources confirm that the statement is a fact. To be considered a fact, a statement must correspond and be coherent with the world in a certain way. For one thing, there must be a set of conditions that would make the statement **not true**. This characteristic of facts is called falsifiability. Facts are the kinds of statements that allow us to reliably predict their falsifiability conditions will *not* occur. If we cannot at least imagine a set of conditions that would lead us to conclude a statement is *false*, then labelling the statement as **true** has no meaning.

The most important thing about the American political system is not whether one party or the other wins or loses an election. Rather, the most important thing about the American political system is that it preserves the set of processes that are most likely to produce fair, unbiased outcomes. Such outcomes recognize the equality, dignity and sanctity of individual persons before the law, regardless of their race, religion, ethnicity, political affiliation, age, gender or sexual orientation.

When former Speaker of the House John Boehner refused to bring a comprehensive immigration reform bill that passed the Senate in June, 2013 to the floor of the House because he was afraid that it had enough bipartisan support to give the Democrats a win, that is not a victory for the Republicans. When the Republican-controlled Senate decided in 2016 that they would not even give the Supreme Court nominee selected by the Democratic president the same procedural justice--a confirmation hearing--granted other Supreme Court nominees, that is not a win for the Republican Party. These are not victories for one political party—they are defeats for the American political system.

The examples above are defeats for the American political process because they deny some American citizens (those with political beliefs other than those held by Republicans) the equal protection of the law. The Constitution says all of us are supposed to be protected equally by the law. But when a majority political party applies the law one way to benefit people who think a certain way, while then changing the standard to deny the same benefit to others, they are abusing their power in a way that should be considered unconstitutional.

The message of my book, *Accountability Citizenship*, is simple. Figure out your values, figure out which candidates best represent those values, and vote for those candidates. I voted early. Tomorrow is election day. Please vote.

CHAPTER 4

You've Been Bubbled: How to Escape the Matrix

Originally published August 14, 2015.

In the classic 1999 science fiction movie, *The Matrix*, most humans live in a completely simulated reality (the Matrix) while their body heat and electricity are harvested to produce power for intelligent machines. The main protagonist, a computer scientist named Neo, is given the opportunity to see reality outside of the simulation when a rebel leader offers him a red pill. Choosing a blue pill, on the other hand, would return Neo to his previous reality. Neo chooses the red pill and the movie progresses through his action-packed fight against the Matrix.

One major premise of *Accountability Citizenship* is that changes in our information environment over the past 50 years have radically changed the skills necessary to process information and formulate reasonable opinions about current events. One doesn't need to imagine a matrix-like conspiracy to acknowledge that deregulation of television and radio, along with the explosion of gadgets from personal computers to cell phones, exponentially increases the amount of information presented to us each day. You might, however, still believe the information that comes to you is random. That is highly unlikely, due to something called a filter bubble.

The filter bubble was first described by Eli Pariser in his best-selling book *The Filter Bubble: How the New Personalized Web is Changing What We Read and How We Think*. Pariser presents examples where different users executing the same search on the same platform are served results that are significantly different, and he asserts the different results are a function of marketing algorithms that essentially create a little structured reality for each of us. There are a wide variety of views about how pervasive or how serious the effects of the filter bubble are on social discourse... and you are probably being served the view that is most consistent with what your personalization algorithm says you will like! (5-8)

Same Day Editions of WSJ with Different Spins for Different Markets
Photo by Stephen Tryon

The picture associated with this essay conveys a slightly more generic version of the filter bubble concept. Several years ago, I was travelling from Salt Lake City to Chicago on business. As I left my house in the morning, I scooped up the Wall Street Journal from my front lawn to read on the plane. Upon arrival at O'Hare, walking to get my bags, I noticed the Wall Street Journal on display had the same graphic but a different headline. On closer examination, I saw there was additional content in the Chicago version of the paper that was not in the version I carried from Salt Lake. The effect of the changes was to make the Utah version of the Wall Street Journal less sympathetic to China and the Chinese government's response to their stock market declines. Someone may have thought the difference in content and tone would affect sales. They may have spun the story to appeal to their perception of what the audience would like.

The problem with filter bubbles is that they feed our bias, and we all have bias. Cognitive bias refers to any systemic pattern of deviation from rationality in judgment. Confirmation bias—a specific type of cognitive bias—is the human psychological tendency to believe things that we *want* to believe. This bias has been shown to distort the way we interpret our experiences to reinforce our preconceptions and conform with our most common or recent prior experiences. By reinforcing confirmation bias, filter bubbles can create a false sense of certainty that can make people less willing to compromise with those who see things differently.

Of course, with a little effort, you can escape the bubble, and AccountabilityCitizenship.org offers you some assistance in this regard. The way out of the bubble is with a relentless pursuit of the facts. As indicated in the quotation from John Adams at the beginning of this book, facts are indeed stubborn things. For all things, we should actively seek a foundation of facts that has not been selected for us by someone else.

The book *Accountability Citizenship* suggests a methodology for building such a foundation, along with a number of reasonably impartial sources of information. The web site itself strives to be such a source, presenting both sides of most issues we cover in our newsletters and being clear about our biases when we choose to present an opinion.

Go ahead, take the pill. We need you out here...

CHAPTER 5

Time, Money and Equality of Opportunity

Time is money... and therefore freedom
Photo by Stephen Tryon

Originally published January 1, 2019.

It's hard to avoid thinking about time on New Year's Day. Arguably, time is the most valuable commodity. We cannot buy more time. We all have 24 hours in a day. When we lack control over what we do during those 24 hours, we say we lack freedom.

We can lack control because we are constrained by external forces-- we can be enslaved or imprisoned or coerced by a despotic government. The Constitution of the United States is a framework for enabling freedom. At the outset, the Constitution did not perfectly provide formal freedom--the freedom enabled by government institutions--to all segments of our population. Freedoms were unjustly restricted based on race, color, gender and economic status. The history of our country has been marked by a history of extending formal freedom to ever-increasing segments of our population.

Formal freedom has never translated to actual freedom immediately. Even after the Constitution was amended to eliminate slavery and extend basic civil rights to people of color and, later, to women, those rights were denied and restricted by informal social mechanisms, domestic terrorism, and procedures specifically designed to obstruct the actual practice of basic freedoms by targeted groups. For these groups, the basic freedoms only became real in practice when sufficient numbers of individuals in society accepted and stood up for the rights of the targeted groups. In other words, the structures of our government enabled freedoms, but only individual behaviors made them real.

And it is also true that, while we cannot buy time, we can buy more control over the time we have. We can buy the services of other people to do tasks we would rather not do, giving us more choice in how we spend our time. In other words, we can buy more freedom. To a certain extent, if your ability to buy more freedom is strictly a function of your positive individual choices and behaviors, I say good for you.

But none of us are strictly a product of our individual choices and behaviors--we all inherit resources or liabilities from our parents. And to the extent that your ability to enjoy more freedom than others is a function of systemic inequality, I say the government has a role in lessening the disparity between the freedom enjoyed by the wealthiest and the freedom allowed to the poorest. That is what the beginning of the Constitution means:

> We the People of the United States, in Order to form a more perfect Union, establish Justice, insure domestic Tranquility, provide for the common defense, promote the general Welfare, and secure the Blessings of Liberty to ourselves and our Posterity, do ordain and establish this Constitution for the United States of America. ("The Constitution" 1)

We cannot say that our government is living up to its constitutional mandates to establish justice and secure the blessings of liberty if it enables too great a disparity between rich and poor. Such a disparity is no less than a disparity between the freedom of the wealthiest and the freedom of the poorest. That disparity violates the letter and spirit of the Constitution, at least to the extent that it is a function of systemic inequality rather than individual merit.

This is not an argument for communism or for any naive utopian concept of economic equality—those philosophies remove the incentive for individual choices and behaviors that are the engine of a productive human society. It is, however, an argument for reasonable constraints on capitalism. Such constraints clearly include a progressive income tax. The purpose of such a tax is not merely to pay for the same set of government services for each citizen, but also to narrow the inequalities in the initial conditions between children born to the rich and children born to the poor.

In his classic book *A Theory of Justice*, John Rawls offers the most elegant defense of this idea. He states it as follows: "Social and economic inequalities are to be arranged so that they are both (a) to the greatest benefit of the least advantaged and (b) attached to offices and positions open to all under conditions of fair equality of opportunity." (Rawls 83) Progressive income taxes support Rawls' vision as well as the purposes enumerated at the beginning of the Constitution.

Progressive taxes do not take away from the freedom of rich children. Rich children do not choose or earn the circumstances of their birth families. Progressive taxation can, however, enhance the freedom of poor children by giving those born to the poorest parents a reasonably level playing field from which to exercise the power of individual choice.

Even though we live in a society that maintains a facade of progressive income taxes, we do not actually enforce those taxes. That is why Senator Romney pays 15 percent of his income in taxes [disclosed in the 2016 campaign and reported in the Salt Lake Tribune] when his actual tax bracket requires something more along the lines of a 34 percent tax payment. For at least the past forty years or so, we have followed a path of empowering an aristocracy of hereditary wealth that is inconsistent with the principles of our Constitution. Ironically, the increasing disparity between rich and poor is reducing the incentives for constructive individual choices and behaviors at both ends of the spectrum.

Constructive individual behavior is key to the freedom of others in society, but it is also the key to our own personal freedom. Destructive behaviors can trap us in the slavery of addiction, debt or hate. These forms of slavery affect all of us without regard for color, race, gender or economic status. We can only liberate ourselves from these forms of self-imposed slavery by making wise choices, and a lot of those choices have to do with how we spend our time.

There are, of course, other factors in our imperfect society. I have argued in this essay for the government's role in mitigating matters of health and circumstance that overwhelm the power of individual choice. I wish you all freedom from such circumstance. I wish you all the opportunity to leverage the power of your choices in the coming year to give yourselves the greatest possible freedom. I wish you all the satisfaction of knowing, on the next New Year's Day, that you have spent your time as wisely as possible this year.

CHAPTER 6

Institutional Racism and Sexism in America

A Historical Puzzle
Photo by Stephen Tryon

Originally published July 25, 2020.

It should not come as a surprise to anyone when I assert that institutional racism and sexism were baked into the original fabric of the United States. I don't state that as an advocate for so-called "cancel culture." I am not lamenting it or judging it in any way. I am simply stating a fact as a starting point in this essay. My moral view of that fact is irrelevant to the purpose of this essay. In this essay, I will use the fact that the government of the United States was born as a racist, sexist institution as support for my conclusion: that institutional racism and sexism still exist in the United States, albeit to a lesser degree, and that the continued manifestations of institutional racism and sexism in 2020 should be morally intolerable for all Americans.

I don't think any reasonable person can deny my starting point. Look at the picture of the signing of the Constitution. The only people in the picture are white men.

Read the words of the original Constitution. They very clearly allow slavery, and the continuation of importing slaves, and the counting of slaves as "three fifths" of a person for purposes of representation in Congress. "Indians not taxed" are excluded from being counted for purposes of representation. Ironically, women are not mentioned. Presumably, because the Declaration only states that "all Men are created equal," the authors of the Constitution did not feel it necessary to explicitly address women. But the Constitution effectively denies equal rights to all three classes—slaves, Indians, and women. That is clear because it requires separate amendments and laws in the nineteenth and twentieth centuries to abolish slavery and grant equal rights to former slaves, Indians, women and people of color. It is a simple fact, therefore, that the political and social institutions of the United States were racist and sexist at the time of the drafting and ratification of the Constitution ("The Constitution", pp. 1-34).

Those who hold that there is no institutional racism and sexism in the United States today must, therefore, believe that something has happened since the drafting and ratification of the Constitution that has removed the original problem. Indeed, we can point to the XIIIth, XIVth, and XVth Amendments to the Constitution as ending slavery, affording equal protection of the law to all persons, and explicitly granting former slaves the right to vote in 1865, 1868, and 1870, respectively. But clearly, this change to the supreme positive law of the United States did not guarantee compliance at the level of state laws and practices.

The 100 years after the Civil War were full of examples of domestic terrorism and murder against African Americans. The federal government effectively looked the other way as the Constitution was ignored in some cases and addressed with inadequate half measures to preserve segregation in others. Violence sometimes erupted into major incidents like white mobs leveling the "Black Wall Street" in Tulsa, Oklahoma in 1921 or the black town of Rosewood, Florida in 1923.

Women and Native Americans saw their rights formally recognized in the XIXth Amendment (1920) and the Indian Citizenship Act (1924), respectively. In practice, these changes in law did not magically change the treatment of women and Native Americans in every aspect of society. Social prejudices persist even when laws change.

When programs like the New Deal, the GI Bill and Veterans home loans seemed to promise economic advancement without regard to race, social practices and governmental policies ensured a preservation of the status quo in a way that systemically took advantage of African Americans and other people of color, holding them at a lower level of economic achievement. Social Security was originally designed to exclude farm workers and domestic workers—exclusions that disproportionately affected black Americans. In 1950, "the National Association of Real Estate Boards' code of ethics warned that 'a Realtor should never be instrumental in introducing into a neighborhood... any race or nationality, or any individuals whose presence will clearly be detrimental to property values." The federal government's Home Owners' Loan Corporation was an active participant in preserving these racial restrictions (Coates 185-88).

The period from 1954 to 1964 saw another series of major changes to public law that seemed to signal real progress towards a society that was not racist. In *Brown v. Board of Education* (1954), the Supreme Court ruled that state laws segregating public schools were unconstitutional (history.com). The Civil Rights Act of 1964 explicitly specified the equal rights for people of all races that had been systemically denied to people of color previously. Violence erupted in many parts of the country as the federal government sought to enforce these rulings (ballotpedia.org).

Ironically, the states failed to ratify the Equal Rights Amendment (ERA) that was intended to grant constitutional protection against gender discrimination. Congress passed the ERA in 1972, but only 31 states approved the amendment. The Constitution requires three fourths of states to approve an amendment before it is ratified. A version of the ERA is still under consideration.

Changes to existing laws continue to address areas where discrimination surfaces in our society. In the years since passage of the Civil Rights Act of 1964, there have been advances in civil rights on many fronts, including race, gender, sexual orientation and identity. Many who argue that current manifestations of discrimination are not manifestations of systemic or institutional racism or sexism seem to feel that the many legal advances to this point have left only a problem with individuals who are racist or sexist or who act in discriminatory ways. These people seem to feel that, since they ascribe the problem to the individual level, there is no need for broad governmental action to address any perceived institutional racism.

This argument seems wrong to me because there is clear evidence that the effects of our social and governmental systems are still having a disproportionately negative impact on people of color and women. In *Griggs v. Duke Power Co*, the Supreme Court established the concept of "disparate impact" as a standard for determining whether a practice, policy or system was a violation of Title VII of the Civil Rights Act of 1964 (Griggs). In employment, the standard is generally this: any practice that is not job related or a business necessity and that has a disparate impact on the basis of race, color, religion, sex or national origin is proof of discrimination. It seems to me that there is a clear disparate impact of our economic, social and legal systems on people of color and women. We can see this disparate impact in different life expectancies, incarceration rates, and levels of economic attainment. As the cases of George Floyd, Breonna Taylor, and many others make painfully clear, we can see a difference in the rate at which civil authorities use force against people of color. Because the evidence of disparate impact is so clear, we must conclude that our systems and institutions still harbor, foster or tolerate racism and sexism.

There have been many attempts to address racism and sexism with legal changes over the years. None have been successful in addressing the whole problem. The fact is that the institutional problem we are confronting today is different than the problem that erupted in the Civil Rights movement of the twentieth century. The problems that exist in our institutions and across society today may not be as intentional or obvious as those addressed by previous generations. That doesn't mean the problems are not institutional, systemic and serious. The argument from disparate impact indicates that they are all of those things.

The twin tragedies of George Floyd and Breonna Taylor's deaths are but instances of a disturbing pattern that should be morally unacceptable to all Americans. The circumstances surrounding these and similar cases demand that we include a systemic and institutional focus as we address the symptoms of racism and sexism in individuals and in groups. Adopting a zero-tolerance policy on inappropriate use of force, coupled with an expanded role for de-escalation skills, community engagement and support activities seem the minimally acceptable steps to take at the level of our local government, law enforcement and educational institutions.

CHAPTER 7

Tools That Help Us Be Amazing Citizens

Originally published August 22, 2015.

Marcus Hamilton delivered the Day 1 general session keynote at the Society of Human Resource Managers National Conference in Las Vegas in June (#SHRM15). His bottom line: the way to create amazing organizations is to give your team leaders the tools they need to be amazing team leaders.

Hamilton's message is a terrific, fundamental insight that reflects everything I've learned in government and business over the past 30+ years. Performance is personal, and great team leaders know how to bring out the best in the people on their teams. Hamilton's quest is to provide the tools that team leaders use to achieve amazing results.

What kinds of tools do we need to be amazing citizens? How can we make each registered voter believe their contribution is valued and important to the processes of our republic?

The most important tool we need is information, but the information that is broadcast to us is not necessarily the information that will make us amazing citizens. We all like to feel that we are right about issues. Plenty of people are willing to make money catering to this aspect of our ego. The information we receive passively is targeted to cater to our cognitive biases.

Tools for citizens
Photo by Stephen Tryon

If the information served to you is your only source of information, you are likely to become more and more comfortable that your biases are correct. This could make you feel more and more superior to those with whom you disagree:

> But, because they had stars, all the Star-Belly
> Sneetches, would brag, 'We're the best kind of
> Sneetch on the beaches! (Geisel 4)

As Dr. Seuss taught us long ago, the only person who wins by making star-bellied sneetches feel superior is the one selling the stars. So, to be an amazing citizen, start with a commitment to not be a star-bellied sneetch.

In *Accountability Citizenship*, I break this down into the two steps of being appropriately positive and appropriately informed. Simply put: do your best to understand the best arguments for the other side--the side you do not agree with--of every issue. Make a habit of finding sources of information that illuminate the best arguments of the other side rather than sources that present you with a cartoon caricature of those positions.

In a perfect world, our elected representatives would help us with this key step by using their official web sites--the ones we pay for with our tax dollars--to provide real-time polling of registered voters in every congressional district. In the same way we log in to perform banking online, registered voters could securely log in to the web sites of their representatives, record their preferences on a range of issues, and see the results in real time. The sites could serve links to sources of unbiased information, like votesmart.org and opensecrets.org, as well.

Providing an easy source of unbiased information for registered voters would increase participation. I spoke recently with a small group of voting-age people in Nevada. Many confirmed they felt unprepared before the most recent election. Many did not vote because they felt they did not know enough about issues and candidates.

Now it is easy at this point to slip into Star-Belly-Sneetch mode and blame these individuals for not taking steps to learn about issues and candidates. But this doesn't solve the problem. Not all of us are as able or willing to sort through conflicting and confusing candidate messaging to prepare to vote, especially when confronted with legitimately higher priorities like family and job. Not all of us have jobs that allow us equal control over our schedules.

We live in an information age, and we should use available technology to make it easier for more people to be informed citizens rather than just accept the current level of confused, frustrated, and effectively disenfranchised citizens. Unfortunately, too many of our elected representatives have a vested interest in preserving the culture of star-bellied sneetches. They represent star-sellers more than they represent the people in their districts.

There are, of course, exceptions. Congressman E. Scott Rigell of Virginia, for instance, was one of a very few members who not only made efforts to survey constituents, but also to share the results of those surveys. The "sense of the district" polls he ran were low-tech and did not provide the kind of real-time feedback that is possible today, but I thought Congressman Rigell's initiative noteworthy.

Unsurprisingly, Rigell was only in Congress a few years, and came to politics after a successful business career and service as a U.S. Marine. Rigell left Congress after a few terms. He is a career citizen, not a career politician.

I believe the responsibility to vote is an individual duty. That is why I called my book *Accountability Citizenship*. We all must hold ourselves accountable for using the powers given us in the Constitution to shape our government. But that doesn't mean our elected officials should not be doing everything in their power to increase accessibility and partic016ipation in the democratic processes of our republic. If our representatives cannot represent all of us on this most fundamental guarantee of our Constitution, how can we trust them to represent any of us on anything?

CHAPTER 8

There is Too Much Dark Money in Politics

Originally published April 9, 2014.

In the spring of 2014, the Supreme Court ruled that the 38-year-old individual cap on total campaign contributions was a violation of First Amendment rights to free speech. In *McCutcheon v. FEC*, the majority opinion relies on three premises (McCutcheon).

First, the ruling holds that political contributions are "speech" in the sense that speech is protected by the Constitution. Second, because political contributions are speech, any limit on the total amount of money allowed for one individual to contribute during a campaign cycle is a restriction on freedom of speech. Third, that restriction is not necessary to preserve the rights of other Americans. All three premises are unsound.

Show me the money!
Stephen Tryon

Political contributions are not speech in the sense that speech is protected by our Constitution. In fact, political contributions are completely different kinds of things than constitutionally protected speech.

Political contributions are money. Money is an inherently constrained resource. The vast majority of Americans never have as much money as they want or need.

Constitutionally protected speech, as an extension of a universal natural right to liberty and the pursuit of happiness, is and must be inherently unconstrained. I can say as many things as I wish; there is no monetary cost to me for my words. I do not have to budget my words.

The vast majority of Americans have limited access to money and unimpeded access to an unlimited supply of words. I can write words on a piece of scrap paper, and it doesn't cost me anything. I cannot take that scrap paper to the store and use it to buy groceries in the same way I can use a $20 bill to buy groceries. To say that there is no difference between a political contribution and the speech protected by our Constitution is like saying that there is no difference between a $20 bill and a piece of paper holding my written words.

This is, of course, an absurd conclusion. We must, therefore, conclude that there is a difference between political contributions and political speech. A restriction on contributions is not the same as a restriction on freedom of speech.

In his majority opinion, Justice Roberts argues that the free speech protected by the Constitution protects many things commonly found objectionable. Each of the examples that he cites, however, is an example of a thing that is relatively unconstrained. By extending the Constitutional protection of speech to money, Justice Roberts conflates two entirely different kinds of things.

Even if political contributions are speech in the sense intended in the Constitution, it is likely that some restriction on an individual's total political contributions is necessary in order to preserve equal protection of the laws for all Americans. No individual rights are absolute. We commonly talk as if they are, but that is clearly wrong. Freedom of religion, for instance, does not extend so far as to protect a religion's practice of human sacrifice.

Generally, we hold that one individual's exercise of her constitutional rights is limited when that exercise violates the constitutional rights of other individuals. In the case of free speech, for instance, we were all taught in school that our right to free speech does not allow us to yell "Fire!" in a crowded theater when no fire exists. The reasoning behind this common example of the limits of free speech is clear: yelling "Fire!" in a crowded theater creates a threat to the safety of others in the theater, some of whom are likely to be injured in the panic caused by this exclamation.

The purpose of political contributions is to acquire access and influence with those who can affect public laws and policy. Allowing unlimited contributions essentially allows unlimited influence on public law to the very few Americans wealthy enough to make the highest contributions. Such unlimited influence violates the equal protection clause of the Constitution and is therefore injurious to the vast majority who do not have the resources to make large political contributions.

Senator John McCain, co-sponsor of the comprehensive McCain-Feingold campaign finance reform legislation, said the Supreme Court's ruling in *McCutcheon v. FEC* undermines laws put in place to protect against corruption. He was correct. Now we need either new legislation to restore those protections, or a class action lawsuit to enable the Court to reconsider this poorly reasoned ruling.

I volunteer to be plaintiff number one.

Study Questions and Key Terms

STUDY QUESTIONS

1. What is the thesis of Essay 5? What reasons does the author give to support this thesis?

2. Do you agree or disagree with the thesis of Essay 5? Why or why not?

3. Essay 6 refers to the "argument from disparate impact." Write out the premises and conclusion that you think the author means when citing the "argument from disparate impact."

4. The United States Constitution identifies six purposes for the American government (see Essay 5). Pick two of the six purposes and describe a situation in which these two purposes conflict with one another. Discuss how you think the conflict should be resolved.

5. Do you think political contributions should be considered constitutionally protected free speech? Why or why not?

KEY TERMS

1. **fact** - a true statement that is falsifiable and can be shown to correspond to a state of affairs in the world, to cohere with a broader set of true statements, and to enable the accurate prediction that its falsifiability conditions will not occur

2. **falsifiability** – the characteristic of any fact that allows people to know or imagine some set of conditions under which the fact could be proven be a false statement (and hence not a fact). A statement that is not falsifiable is meaningless (and hence not a fact)

3. **fake news** – a term used by President Trump to attack the media and discredit information that is unflattering or damaging to his pre-

ferred narrative, regardless of whether the information labelled as fake news is true

4. **justice** - a state in which individuals are treated fairly; the application of laws to individuals and organizations in an impartial manner regardless of characteristics that have no relation to the behavior controlled by the law; showing proper regard for human rights

5. **filter bubble** – the set of impressions selectively delivered to an individual or group after some assessment of what will most appeal to the cognitive bias of that individual or group

6. **cognitive bias** – any systemic pattern of deviation from rationality in judgment; the evolution of the human brain favored certain patterns of bias that aided survival

7. **confirmation bias** – the human psychological tendency to interpret our experiences to reinforce preconceptions and conform with our most common or recent prior experiences

8. **domestic terrorism** – the use of violence by citizens against other citizens or government agencies to further social, religious, or political agendas or redress perceived grievances; The KKK engaged in widespread domestic terrorism against African Americans to restrict access to the rights of citizenship conferred by the XIIIth, XIVth, and XVth Amendments. The 1995 bombing of the Federal Building in Oklahoma City was an act of domestic terrorism.

9. **race** – a grouping of humans based on shared physical or social qualities

10. **gender** – term used to denote the spectrum of identities reflecting biological, social and cultural distinctions ranging from female to male

11. **sexual orientation** – a person's identity in relation to the gender or genders to which they are sexually attracted

12. **systemic inequalities** – meta-characteristics and processes in society that influence individual opportunities and can lead to disparate social, economic and educational outcomes

13. **progressive income tax** – a system of taxation that requires a higher percentage of income to be paid as taxes by people earning more money than by people earning less money

14. **disparate impact** – something incommensurable; an outcome, usually negative, that is the result of some irrelevant factor and is therefore often considered unjust and in need of remediation
15. **Racism and sexism** – the use of irrelevant characteristics of race or gender to negatively impact the opportunities and rewards for groups sharing certain physical characteristics

PART III

Fix Yourself First

Bottom Line Up Front

The main idea of this section is that each of us has to "fix" our personal bias in order to be good citizens. We all have bias--preconceptions or preferences about how things-in-the-world do or should work. Our bias can act as an internal filter, causing us to project our values on our experiences, regardless of the actual features and relationships contained in those experiences. Filter bubbles (last section) are psychological techniques for using individual bias to sell ideas and products. Together, natural bias and filter bubbles can significantly distort our perception of right conduct or the best solution to a problem (Ch 9). We must have humility to acknowledge our bias and tolerance to accept the ideas of others (Ch 10). Religion and anti-religion are powerful social filters (Ch 11). Our filters can create vicious cycles that poison our relationships with others (Ch 12, 13). Technology can magnify the negative effects of our bias, if we let it (Ch 14, 15).

CHAPTER 9

Understand Your Confirmation Bias

Originally published May 8, 2018.

Cognitive bias refers to any systemic pattern of deviation from rational judgment. Confirmation bias is a particular type of cognitive bias. According to brittanica.com, confirmation bias is "the tendency to process information by looking for, or interpreting, information that is consistent with one's existing beliefs." (brittanica.com) *Psychology Today* states that confirmation bias "confirms the views (prejudices) one would like to be true."

Art and photo by Stephen Tryon

Confirmation bias is involuntary. Our human brains evolved mechanisms for confirmation bias because these mechanisms help us react more quickly (Kahneman 25-27, 80-81). Your experiences have further ingrained biases into your brain (Eberhardt 17-21). For these reasons, when you find yourself in the realm of disagreement, and are trying to reason your way to what is "right," it is important to ask yourself what you would like to be true. In this way, you can activate the parts of your brain that may be able to recognize your personal confirmation bias. This can help you be more objective in reaching your conclusion.

CHAPTER 10

Start with Humility

Originally published February 21, 2019.

I get that we are worried about foreign governments planting misinformation in American social media as a way to influence elections and undermine the processes of our society. Ultimately, however, I am more concerned by the fact that there are large numbers of people unable or unwilling to protect themselves from thinly veiled misinformation. The first step to the truth is to have a proper humility about the things you believe to be true.

Humility
Photo by Stephen Tryon

If you have been paying attention, the concepts of cognitive bias and confirmation bias offer a sound reason for all of us to be humble about our opinions. We have evolved with brains that are built to react quickly. Our brains synthesize information and present conclusions that are not necessarily best supported by all available facts. When we have time, we should choose to be humble and seek ways to mitigate our individual bias. We can do this by being genuinely tolerant of those with different views than our own, acknowledging that different perspectives may offer real value in reaching optimal solutions and outcomes.

Benjamin Franklin's statement on the last day of the Constitutional Convention is one of the best expressions I have encountered of this humility of thought:

> I confess there are several parts of this constitution which I do not at present approve....But I am not sure I will never approve them. For having lived long, I have experienced many instances of being obliged by better information or fuller consideration, to change opinions even on important subjects, which I once thought right, but found to be otherwise. It is therefore that the older I grow, the more apt I am to doubt my own judgment, and to pay more respect to the judgment of others. Most men indeed as well as most sects in religion, think themselves in possession of all truth, and that wherever others differ from them it is so far error.... In these sentiments, Sir, I agree to this Constitution with all its faults, if they are such (Franklin).

Franklin famously believed America could preserve our republic only if the people could live with civic and personal virtue. Adopting an appropriate humility toward one's personal beliefs, along with an appropriate respect for the beliefs of others, is the first step toward this ideal of virtue.

CHAPTER 11

Add Tolerance in Your Search for Truth

Originally published February 18, 2019.

One of the most fascinating aspects of the men who founded our nation is the fact that so many of them were Deists, including George Washington. James Thomas Flexner, in his essential biography of our first President, writes, "Washington subscribed to the religious faith of the Enlightenment: like Franklin and Jefferson, he was a deist." (Flexner, p. 216). Catherine Drinker Bowen, author of *Miracle at Philadelphia-- The Story of the Constitutional Convention May to September 1787*, writes that "Deism was in the air.... Dr. Franklin could have defined this creedless religion; with Jefferson and John Adams, the Doctor shared the Deistical outlook" (216). Washington's religious belief was but one example of his amazing ability to bring reason to bear on the social conventions of his day.

The fascinating thing about the broad popularity of Deism among the luminaries of eighteenth-century America is that it is so rational. Deism, or natural religion, acknowledges the existence of a Supreme Being but, at the same time, acknowledges that we cannot know anything specific about this being. It is the perfect reconciliation of the religious intuition many of us share, with the limits of what we can confirm as fact. While insisting on the existence of a Creator, Deism denies that there is any rational basis for the overly specific dogmas associated with the anthropomorphic mythologies we call--collectively--organized religion. Because there is no rational basis for the differences between the world's organized religions, if you are a Deist, tolerance and freedom of religion are central to your philosophy.

Tolerance
Stephen Tryon

Neither can scientists who insist on fact alone disqualify the religious intuition that so many of us share. That widely shared religious intuition is itself a fact. And there is so much about creation that we simply do not understand. Most of the matter and energy in the universe is "dark"--it does not appear to react with the matter and energy we see. Given all we do not know about the universe, there is nothing irrational about Deism, especially if one pursues it with a spirit of humility and an understanding of confirmation bias.

Among the many exceptional things about our first President was his ability to rise above the constraints and conventions of his world through the application of practical reason. After the death of his father when he was only eleven, George Washington's education was limited to about the eighth-grade level. Yet this man, with no formal military training, became the Commanding General of an army that defeated the most powerful army in the world at the time. This man served as president of the convention that produced our Constitution. By the end of his life, he understood that the institution of slavery was inconsistent with the principles of that Constitution and provided in his will for the emancipation of the slaves at Mount Vernon. This man understood that reason was consistent with his faith in a Supreme Being but was not consistent with the many dogmas and prejudices associated with the common practice of organized religion. We should follow his example, and practice tolerance in our pursuit of truth.

CHAPTER 12

Star Trek Lesson on Beating Hate

Originally published June 28, 2018.

I am a bit of a Star Trek nerd. I've watched every episode of the original series, the "Next Generation" series, and all of the movies. I like the franchise because, like all good fiction, it weaves some powerful messages about common aspects of the human condition into its very uncommon settings. If you pay attention, there are some good lessons to be found in the adventures of the starship Enterprise and its crew. One of my favorite episodes of all is "The Day of the Dove", which aired the first week in November, 1968.

Star Trek, November 1968
Art and photo by Stephen Tryon

For those of you who didn't live that time, let me provide a bit of historical context. The Cold War between the US and the Soviet Union (Russia) was at its height, with both sides armed to the teeth with enough nuclear, chemical and conventional weapons to destroy the world many times over. Proxy "hot wars" were being fought in places like Africa and South America. The Vietnam War was at its height. At home, the Civil Rights Act was just a few years old, and the conflict between the federal government's enforcement of the new law and some state and local efforts to resist it was one source of violence in American cities. Just a year earlier, during the "long hot summer of 1967," racial unrest had led to so much violence in Detroit that the government deployed the 82d Airborne Division and the National Guard to help restore order. There was also conflict between those who were protesting the war in Vietnam and those who insisted we had to support our military.

I think it is safe to say that racial and political tension was higher in 1968 that it had been since Reconstruction. In a span of just over two months in 1968, Martin Luther King was assassinated in Memphis (April 4) and Bobby Kennedy (the Democratic nominee for the 1968 presidential election) was assassinated in Los Angeles (June 6). The episode of Star Trek I am referencing in this blog aired 4 days before the 1968 presidential election.

The lesson of "The Day of the Dove" is simply that hate and violence warp our ability to accurately perceive facts and reality, and that cycles of violence are "vicious cycles" where negative behaviors can reinforce each other and perpetuate--even magnify--the cycle. You can view the trailer for this episode on youtube.com. I wish everyone in our country would take 45 minutes and watch the whole episode (you can download it from Amazon and probably other places as well). I wish everyone would familiarize themselves with the history of this turbulent time in America. Spoiler alert: the crew of the Enterprise join forces with their arch enemies, the Klingons, to defeat a hate monster. They do it by recognizing that hate blinds us, and that we can overcome it if we work to find common ground.

We have a lot of common ground in America. Things are nowhere near as bad today as they were in November 1968. But we should make an effort to celebrate the goodness in our country and what we have in common, even as we work through our disagreements over how to make it even better. We should focus on facts rather than on blind loyalty to this faction or that faction. Beware of any group that tries to prevent you from seeking common ground and understanding with others. Any others. Even the Klingons.

Live long and prosper!

CHAPTER 13

Fix Your Bias on Race: Start by Admitting It's There

Originally published July 18, 2020.

I am going to start this essay by stating, emphatically, that Black Lives Matter.

I acknowledge that systemic racism and sexism exist, that systemic racism and sexism harm people of color and women (in general), and I support the agenda of fixing social systems to eliminate systemic racism and sexism affecting people of color and women. I want to make that perfectly clear at the outset because I am likely to say things in this essay that will offend many people on all sides of these issues. My goal is to be honest, because I believe honesty is the essential element of any solution to challenges like racism and sexism.

I'm sure there are people already offended, so let me address the imaginary conflict between "All Lives Matter" and "Black Lives Matter" right at the outset. In business, we measure programs and processes by outcomes. And here we are, nearly 60 years after the Civil Rights Act was passed, and the outcomes still reflect disparate impact based on race and gender. By every measure I can see, all the programs and processes designed to ensure equal protection of the law to people of color and women are failing. Nowhere is that problem more severe in American society than with the African American community.

African Americans are still suffering from the legacy of slavery in America. Today, in 2020, we find they are still disproportionately poor, disproportionately sick, disproportionately jailed, and disproportionately killed by law enforcement. For that reason alone, it is 100 percent appropriate to focus our efforts on making sure that every segment and every level of our society internalizes the message that Black Lives Matter. The outcomes clearly indicate we have not internalized that message, and the consequences of our failure to do so going forward will be fatal to the American republic, at least insofar as that republic is supposed to represent the fulfillment of the promise of the United States Constitution.

Some will say that the problems are all related to individual choices, and I think that is completely inconsistent with the evidence I see. I have a friend about my age who, like me, is a West Point graduate and a retired infantry officer. He went into a store in downtown Denver a few years ago and security stopped him on the way out so they could check his pockets for stolen merchandise. That has never happened to me, and I suspect it never will. He is black, and I am white.

Remember Harvard professor Henry Louis Gates, Jr.? He was arrested on July 16, 2009 after police responded to a 911 call about an attempted burglary. Gates was just returning from a trip to China and had enlisted the help of his cab driver when he found the front door of his house stuck. What should have been a three-minute conversation with the police resulted in the arrest of a Harvard University professor. I can guarantee that would not have happened if Gates had been white. If you doubt that, read what the Boston police did to Jennifer Eberhardt the day before she received her Ph.D. from Harvard (Eberhardt 98-101). In these three cases, distinguished individuals with a record of making great choices were harassed unnecessarily because they were black.

Some will correctly point out that the three cases I cite in the preceding paragraphs provide only anecdotal evidence for my thesis. Here's some more anecdotal evidence: Watch the video of George Floyd being murdered by police. Watch the video of Terence Crutcher being murdered by police. Read about how Philando Castile was stopped for a broken taillight and then shot to death in the front seat of a car in which his girlfriend and her four-year old daughter were passengers. Read about how Breonna Taylor's apartment was targeted and broken into by police, resulting in Breonna being shot and killed. Read about the 2015 Charleston church massacre where nine African Americans were murdered by a white supremacist during a Bible study. Read about the 2017 neo-Nazi and white supremacist rally in Charlottesville, Virginia. You could keep reading and watching for a long time, but at some point, you should just stop and consider the statistics. What is clear is that there is an overwhelming amount of evidence that we have a serious race-relations problem in the United States, that the policies intended to solve that problem have failed, and that we all—regardless of our race—have both individual and collective duties to do something to fix the problem.

Racism

I begin this discussion of racism at the individual level by reminding the reader of what I have said in a previous essay about bias in general: we all have it, whether our skin color is white, black, brown, yellow or red. It's part of how we are constructed as homo sapiens. A recent training on implicit bias cited a statistic from a Harvard University study: our brains process approximately 11 million pieces of information every second, and we can only process about 40 of those consciously. Daniel Kahneman's excellent book *Thinking Fast and Slow* is a superb overview of how our minds use models to simplify what we experience and how our models are biased by experience, emotion and evolutionary factors.

Implicit bias does not have to cause racism. We can define racism as discrimination or antagonism directed against others because of their race or ethnicity. Another definition that I like is based on outcomes: racism is whatever perpetuates inequality that persists on racial lines.

Our first duty as individuals in combatting racism is to force ourselves to consciously surface and interrogate our propensities, likes and dislikes to try and understand our bias. Stanford social psychologist Jennifer L. Eberhardt, Ph.D., presents this and other ways to combat bias in her book *Biased: Uncovering the Hidden Prejudice That Shapes What We See, Think and Do* (285-93).

Diversity
Photo by Stephen Tryon

Forcing ourselves to be aware of our bias is especially important when making decisions that affect others. Building systems with checks and balances helps. We are social animals—we should seek the input of others to mitigate our personal bias wherever possible. This does not mean we cannot make individual decisions. It does mean we are likely to make better decisions when we consider the perspectives of others.

Another duty in combatting racism is to confront it, peacefully and persistently, when we see it. We should all insist that the people around us show proper respect for others, in word and deed. We should never tolerate disrespectful language or conduct based on race, ethnicity, religion, gender, sexual identity or orientation.

Once, shortly after taking over management of a warehouse (and publishing my expectations for all employees), I discovered an employee had used a racial slur—directed at an Asian co-worker—on our hand-held radio network. I immediately contacted the supervisor to bring the employee to my office so I could fire him. The team arrived with the Asian co-worker as well, who insisted it was all a joke. He assured me he was not offended. I told him that the behavior was clearly against my policy, and that the behavior offended me. Then I fired the employee who had used the slur. All of us, especially when we are leaders (but even when we are not), must confront racist behavior. It is far too easy for people to rationalize bad conduct under the guise of friendship or team-work.

White Privilege

In the introduction to my 2013 book *Accountability Citizenship*, I wrote "For both my father and myself, I see a combination of both hard work and luck as the main features of a tapestry spanning nearly one hundred years.... I am the American dream fulfilled." If you would have asked me then what I meant by "luck," I would have said that I was lucky to have had the parents and siblings that I have, I was lucky in my military career to have survived a few near misses, and I was lucky to have met the future CEO of the company where I would eventually go to work. If you would have then asked me what I thought about the role race played in any person's ability to live the American dream, I would have said something about the Civil Rights Act and the progress that we have made since then. I would have concluded that racism was still a problem in some places, but, by and large, people of all races could achieve the same level of success with the same amount of hard work and luck. And I would have been wrong.

I now think that answer is incomplete, because I now believe that part of the "luck" that enabled my success was what people are now re-ferring to as white privilege. I have rewritten that sentence a few times. I want to be absolutely clear that I do not believe any race is superior to any other race. I have never sought preferential treatment based on my race, and have always taken pride in earning my way based on my skills and merit. I would never have approved of a system that gave me an ad-vantage because of the color of my skin, especially if that system disad-vantaged others because their skin color was different. But regardless of all that, it is now clear to me that American society, in general, even in 2020, offers a multitude of advantages to white people that are not avail-able to people of color. I have benefited from the white cultural orientation of American society. That is to say, I have benefited from white privilege.

I believe we all have a duty to work toward a society where no one is privileged based on the color of their skin. At the same time, given the failures of policies and programs designed to produce equitable outcomes for Americans of all races, I do not think we are anywhere close to a society that can function fairly without government oversight programs like Affirmative Action. In addition to the duties to combat racism mentioned earlier in this essay, it is my individual responsibility to articulate the need for such programs, to participate in the dialogue about how to make them effective, and to use my vote to support racial justice.

It is our duty to make a reasonable effort to understand diverse perspectives. We can do this by reading, through dialogue, voluntary exposure to cultural events sponsored by those with different backgrounds, and by sharing elements of our own heritage. These individual duties apply to people of every race. Even if kids are more comfortable sitting with other kids that look like them in the school cafeteria, all kids should make an effort to include people of all races in their social circles. The fact that this may be uncomfortable for some makes it even more important.

The Roots of Racial Inequality Are Older than the United States

Years ago, textbooks rationalized colonialism, conquest and exploitation of indigenous populations with the argument that the conquering powers brought technology and improvements to the quality of life of the conquered people. Buried in this proposition was the assumption that native peoples were somehow inferior to the conquerors, adding a racist rationale to the raw profit motive of economic exploitation. The racist notion that colonialism was a duty to lift up people of color was known as the "white man's burden."

The question of why technology and social organizations grew at different rates among different peoples is a reasonable line of inquiry. To paraphrase the words of UCLA Professor Jared Diamond, why did Europeans arrive to conquer the Incas rather than the Incas arriving to conquer Spain? In *Guns, Germs and Steel—The Fates of Human Societies*, Diamond provides an excellent description of how environmental factors shaped the speed with which civilizations emerged, developed various technologies, and projected their power on other peoples.

First, and most importantly, Diamond provides a clear rationale for why human societies developed at different speeds that debunks the racist idea that white Europeans developed faster due to inherent superiority.

> In short, Europe's colonization of Africa had nothing to do with differences between European and African peoples themselves, as white racists assume. Rather, it was due to accidents of geography and biogeography—in particular to the continents' different areas, axes, and suites of wild plant and animal species (401).

Guns, Germs and Steel offers a fascinating and comprehensive analysis of these factors across all regions and peoples.

Diamond makes the case that homo sapiens moved more rapidly from hunter-gatherer societies to agriculture-based societies in areas where there were higher concentrations of wild plants and animals suitable for domestication and food production. In turn, the ability to generate a surplus of food in a reliable fashion enabled the rise of cities, classes of people who could focus on something other than survival, armies, and technology. Population-dense groups living in proximity with domesticated animals suffered from new forms of communicable disease, to which many developed immunities. All together, these factors gave farming societies the ability to expand, displacing or conquering hunter-gatherer societies in their path.

Second, Diamond points out that the pattern of expansion, conquest, displacement, enslavement and brutalization of conquered peoples occurs all over the world among all the races of homo sapiens. For example, the Bantu expansion in Africa, the empires of Mesoamerica and South America, and the expansion of societies in Asia and the Pacific all ended badly for the people who were conquered and displaced. Just as being conquered does not imply intellectual inferiority, neither does it confer moral superiority. Power corrupts, it seems. Across all races, people with the power to expand, conquer and dominate their neighbors have done so.

The differentiator, according to Diamond, is the original "luck" that accrued to peoples living in areas with sufficient biodiversity to give them a head start on the path to guns, germs and steel. These peoples moved more rapidly to the stage of expansion and conquest by virtue of the geographical and ecological factors of their original homeland. Therefore, we can say that "white privilege" has its roots in a much older "Fertile Crescent privilege." Neither privilege was ever deserved, earned, or intended by most of the people they have affected (positively or negatively).

The problem with white privilege in the United States lies primarily in areas where we can see that privilege has been leveraged, extended and caused to persist through injustice and with intention. Those of us who have remained unaware of privilege, as well as those who have passively accepted it, are also at fault when we refuse to acknowledge the disparate impacts evident in the most basic statistics about our society. It is far past time for a comprehensive evaluation of social systems and processes to achieve justice for all.

Conclusion

Racism—defined as either discrimination directed against others on the basis of their race or whatever perpetuates inequality that persists on racial lines—is evil. It arises from bias. We all have bias, and we should acknowledge that fact. But bias does not become racism until we either engage in or tolerate unjust behavior. It is our duty as citizens of the United States to ensure our personal conduct neither creates nor enables racism in any form.

CHAPTER 14

Fix Your Sources of Information

Originally published November 26, 2020.

There are two key elements to ensuring that you are properly informed: (1) consult a range of sources that span the spectrum of perspectives on key issues, and (2) ensure the sources that you consult are reputable sources of news.

Choose Reasonable Sources
Collage by Stephen Tryon

In order to have an intelligent opinion on any subject, you must be able to respond intelligently to criticisms of that argument. You cannot respond intelligently to criticisms of your position unless you understand how people with different perspectives view your position. To gain this understanding, you must listen to sources that present those perspectives fairly, honestly and in the best possible light.

Fifty years ago, you could turn from one news program to another on the three major networks and get basically the same perspective on the news. Now, there are far more than three options for news. Each source is likely to have its own editorial slant. The stories that are emphasized are often completely different, and the editorial slant given to the common stories are likely to be completely different.

Sometimes there are good reasons for different media outlets to offer different perspectives on the same issue. After all, there are different ways of identifying the correct or optimal solution to any given challenge. As discussed in previous essays, we can identify different approaches to any issue—constitutional perspectives, arguments from various moral or religious perspectives, and efficiency arguments. All may have merit while yielding different solutions.

Because sources of news have become more politicized and polarized, it is necessary to consult multiple, reputable sources across the spectrum to get a fair and honest portrayal of opinions contrary to your own. It is often hard to watch programs that present the opposing view, but you should make a practice of monitoring news as it is portrayed by media outlets that make you uncomfortable. Take note of the stories they cover that your favorite channels do not cover, as well as how their coverage of common stories differs.

Reputable news sources are sources that do not deal in falsehoods. If you are watching or reading a news source that continually broadcasts or publishes stories that are subsequently identified as misleading or false, then you should find a higher quality source for news. Often such sources are labelled as "tabloids" rather than newspapers.

Some of my recommended sources for serious news are the Wall Street Journal, the New York Times, the Washington Post, The Economist, both the broadcasts and website for NPR.org, and the BBC.com. You will often find this set of sources will cover the same major stories. These sources are world famous, have different owners, and have a reason to preserve their credibility as a source of their competitive advantage. For that reason, you can often use these sources to judge the quality of other media outlets, and to identify significant omissions or editorial slants.

Surveying coverage over a range of media outlets can also help hone your skills at identifying better and worse quality in media outlets. For instance, you can get a liberal slant on stories by watching CNN and a conservative slant by watching Fox News. When you compare coverage with a magazine like The Economist or an outlet like NPR.org, you are likely to notice when CNN and Fox spend their time covering different stories. You will notice when they give very different perspectives on issues and personalities, and develop a feel for what is more likely to be true.

In sum, broadening the scope of your news intake to cover a range of sources will make you a better-informed citizen. You will be more prepared to defend your opinions because you will be familiar with opposing views. Over time, you will build up your ability to discern quality in media coverage of current events.

CHAPTER 15

Remember the Krell &
Stay Positive

Originally published November 22, 2019.

The 1956 science fiction classic *Forbidden Planet* projects the plot of Shakespeare's *Tempest* into outer space, and makes that brilliant plot accessible to all of us. A young Leslie Nielsen leads a rescue expedition to a distant planet only to find the sole survivors of the previous mission unwilling to accept their help and unable to explain the deaths of the rest of their party. Walter Pidgeon plays the scientist father engrossed in the study of the Krell—the extinct super-race that once inhabited the forbidden planet. We learn this super-race had invented technology that magnified their mental capacity, enabling them to reach unimaginable technological achievements.

Art and Photo by Stephen Tryon

Eventually, we learn that the same technology that propelled them to great achievement ultimately destroyed the Krell. Only the dying words of one of Nielsen's crew gives the critical insight: Krell technology not only magnified their positive mental capability, but also their negative, violent emotions as well.

Hopefully, you have a sense of deja vu when you consider the amazing advances we have experienced in the information age. Without a doubt, information technology has greatly accelerated the technological achievement of the human race. In just the last 50 years, we have gone from putting the first humans on the moon to mass marketing cell phones that give almost all of us more computing power than the Apollo 11 space ship. Starting around 20 years ago, we began producing more bytes of information every few days than was produced in the entire history of human kind previously. Advances in medicine, artificial intelligence, transportation and communications propel our human species at a dizzying pace. Yet, for all of the power of our technology, we seem helpless to stop the destructive side of our technology. Nowhere is this truer than in the realm of social media, where we seem to have lost our ability to treat each other civilly, to disagree without letting our differences fuel hatred and division, and to tell the difference between truth and deception.

I will resist the temptation to call for some mechanism to curb the evil effects of our technology. The lesson is all too clear. From Shakespeare to *Forbidden Planet*, the solution to the challenges of power is not to be found in magic or in the next technological leap forward. The basic challenge is to balance the allure of an ever-more-powerful independent individualism with the irresistible force of our nature as social animals.

They say the largest organism on our planet is either the pando "forest of one tree" in Utah or the Armillaria ostoyae fungus in Oregon. The forest seems to consist of over 47,000 individual aspen trees, but in fact shares one massive underground root system. Similarly, the so-called humongous fungus in Oregon is connected mostly under the surface of the ground--its visible manifestations appear to be discrete individual clusters of mushrooms that bloom in the autumn. In both cases, the appearance of individuals is an illusion, and we can confirm the connection that exists beneath the surface. In both cases, however, the health of the organism as a whole depends on protecting the health of the connective tissue.

In the case of our species, I think it is perfectly reasonable to note that the sense we have of our individual existence is largely an illusion--the "roots" that connect us are our thoughts, and we have never been more connected as a species than we are today. The challenge lies in the fact that thoughts and the media through which we share them are not physical, and can just as easily spread poison as nutrition. It is up to each of us to tend to the portion of the root system that we touch: to be respectful, kind, honest, and to demand the same from those around us. Ultimately, we are indeed affected by and connected to our fellow creatures. It is less important to be right or to win as an individual than it is to support the growth of the community you inhabit.

Study Questions and Key Terms

1. We all have bias. Discuss an area where you believe your confirmation bias may interfere with your ability to accept or evaluate information. What steps can you take to mitigate your bias?

2. Does the Constitution of the United States contain mechanisms that help us mitigate the confirmation bias of individual political leaders as we make national decisions? Why or why not?

3. Identify at least four sources of national and international news. Discuss why you feel these sources are (a) reputable, and (b) provide adequate coverage of the spectrum of opinion.

4. What is the thesis of Essay 10? What reasons does the author give to support this thesis? Write out the reasons and the thesis in the form of an argument (premises and conclusion).

5. Essay 12 describes the plot of an episode of Star Trek. What is the moral of this episode? Construct a deductive argument with this moral as its conclusion.

6. In Essay 13, the author argues that systemic racism and sexism still exist in American society today (2021). Write out the author's argument for this conclusion. Can you identify any premises that are themselves the conclusions of arguments that rely on inductive reasoning?

1. **Deism** - belief in the existence of a supreme creator, usually associated with Enlightenment thinkers who rejected much of the dogma and superstition tied to popular religions
2. **Civil War** – war between northern (union) and southern (confederate) US states over slavery that began with the confederate attack on Fort Sumter, SC (April 12, 1861) and ended with the confederate surrender at Appomattox Courthouse (April 9, 1865)
3. **Civil Rights Act of 1964** - landmark law that makes discrimination based on race, color, religion, sex, national origin and (later) sexual orientation illegal;
4. **Cold War** - period of global geopolitical tension and competition between the Soviet Union and the United States and their respective allies. Often cast as the global struggle between communism and capitalism; marked by regional "hot" wars like the Vietnam War.
5. **Vietnam War** - war between United States and North Vietnam (1955 – 1975) that resulted in the unification of Vietnam under the North Vietnamese communist government.
6. **white privilege** - the benefits (including the absence of racial profiling and unfair treatment experienced by people of color) afforded by the cultural orientation of American society to the majority Caucasian populace
7. **hunter-gatherer** - nomadic people who live by hunting, fishing and harvesting wild food
8. **indigenous people** - communities associated with geographically distinct, traditional territories that identify themselves as descendants of groups present in the territory before modern states and borders
9. **biogeography** - area of biology concerning geographical distribution of plants and animals
10. **injustice**- unfair treatment; systemic or arbitrary application of laws and awarding of social benefits in an unfair manner or based on irrelevant characteristics

11. **editorial slant** - the perspective favored by the author or presenter of information, usually resulting from the omission or devaluation of information supporting other perspectives
12. **reputable source** - source that acknowledges their editorial slant, is transparent about alternative perspectives, and offers sound reasons for its editorial choices
13. **assumption** - something accepted as true without independent factual support, often in the context of building support for some other assertion; e.g. "A weak assumption can undermine the credibility of your conclusion."
14. **technology** - a practical application of scientific knowledge; e.g., mobile phone or internet
15. **social media** - websites and applications that enable users to create and share content or to network in various ways.

PART IV

Facts and Fake News

Bottom Line Up Front

The main idea of this section is to present a *practical* foundation for knowing whether something is true or false. First, we discuss reasonable limits to the virtues of humility and tolerance in the age of QAnon (Ch 16). We often refer to true statements as facts. "Fake news" has become synonymous with statements we believe to be false. People use these terms to describe statements they like as facts. Statements they do not like are fake news. But our personal likes and dislikes have nothing to do with whether a statement is true or false (Ch 17). A rational framework for truth includes two attributes: (1) correspondence with the world of experience, or coherence with other verifiable facts (or both correspondence and coherence); and (2) falsifiability. Falsifiability, in turn, can be viewed as the inverse of verifiability, and has attributes of repeatability and predictability (Ch 18-21). Ockham's Razor is a 700-year-old standard identifying theories using the fewest assumptions (aka ad hoc hypotheses) as the most likely to be true (Ch 22). The final essays apply truth standards to evaluate assertions from recent news (Ch 23, 24).

CHAPTER 16

The Limits of Humility and Tolerance

Originally published February 22, 2019.

Humility and tolerance are important virtues for any free society, but, in this age of information and misinformation, they are not absolutes.

Benjamin Franklin's excellent statement on the final day of the Constitutional Convention, which we considered in the last section, reflects a healthy humility and respect for the views of others (Franklin). In *Apology*, Plato describes Socrates as holding that the greatest wisdom was to know that you know nothing. With all due respect to Socrates, I think he takes things a bit too far (probably just as a rhetorical device).

We can know things. We do know things. How do we differentiate between what we know and what we merely think we know? How do we balance humility with knowledge?

Rene Descartes was a French philosopher, soldier, mathematician, and scientist. He lived in the first half of the 17th century (1596-1650). In his *Discourses and Essays*, Descartes offers a simple argument to start us back on the path to establishing what we can know.

Descartes set about a thought experiment, examining everything he thought he "knew", and imagining whether it was possible that some powerful wizard was simply deceiving him about this knowledge. He determined that there was one fact about which the wizard could not deceive him--the fact of his existence. Descartes reasoned that, even if everything in his experience was simply an illusion, he himself--the entity that was experiencing the illusion--had to exist. Stated another way, the powerful wizard had to be deceiving something with his illusions, and that something had to exist. Descartes summarized his conclusion with the famous statement, "I am thinking, therefore I exist" (Descartes 127).

Descartes' conclusion immediately forces us to confront a critical question: who is this "I" that exists? Each of us answers that question for ourselves, consciously or by default. There are, however, some necessary elements in the equation. Humans have an irreducible social component to our nature, along with evolved mechanisms for rationalizing and protecting our self-interest.

I think therefore I am
Photo by Stephen Tryon

Striking an appropriate balance between our social nature and our self-interest enables a reasonable limit to intellectual humility. For example, we do not have to shy away from asserting that lying, law-breaking and enabling others to break the law are almost always morally wrong because they undermine the fabric of trust necessary for a healthy society. In the absence of extraordinary circumstances, our duty to be truthful and law-abiding is a logical consequence of our nature as social animals. Humility does not imply moral relativism.

Just as humility has limits, so too does tolerance. The best practical expression of the limits of tolerance for our society may be this passage from the Fourteenth Amendment to the U.S. Constitution.

> No state shall make or enforce any law which shall
> abridge the privileges or immunities of citizens of
> United States; nor shall any State deprive any person
> of life, liberty, or property, without due process of
> law; nor deny to any person within its jurisdiction
> the equal protection of the laws ("The Constitution" 25-26).

In essence, these words tell us that we shall not tolerate three types of state laws: laws that deny *any person* the equal protection of the law; laws that deprive *any person* of life, liberty or property without due process of law; and laws that limit any of the rights reserved for *citizens of the United States*. Similarly, the first ten amendments to our Constitution establish things we shall not tolerate with regard to actions of the federal government.

Thus, the explicit statement of our social contract places specific limits on the virtue of tolerance. These limits are positive law. They protect individual rights from encroachment by government.

We should add another limit on the virtue of tolerance in order to put reasonable controls on the transmission of false and misleading information. The challenge is to establish controls that improve the quality of information in the public domain without censorship. We can meet this challenge with systematic, voluntary badging for organizations and sources that are in the business of providing information to the public.

Establishing a business is a regulated process. Businesses are assigned entity numbers that aid in taxation. In the United States, registered businesses also use the North American Industry Classification System (NAICS), which labels businesses based on types of economic activity. Independent Artists, Writers and Publishers, for instance, use NAICS code 7115. It would be a relatively simple matter to identify the businesses that should be subject to the voluntary badging protocol.

All businesses identified as in scope would either have to apply for a voluntary, annual certification process or label their websites and publications with a specified warning label ("The content of this source has not been certified as conforming to the standards of truthfulness endorsed by the United States Government. Consumers should exercise caution with regard to accepting or transmitting information from this source."). Businesses that pass the certification could display an official badge proclaiming that they have been certified as conforming to accepted standards for truthfulness. The source of certification could either be the government (at any level: local state or federal) or a business council comprised of representative industry players.

The certification could be based on simple, accepted standards such as correspondence, coherence and falsifiability, and it could be given with an appropriate disclaimer specifying how much content was audited, the date of the last audit, and the percentage of audited content that met the truthfulness standard. The disclaimer would further state that sponsored content was not audited, but was required to be labelled as sponsored content. Businesses could be subject to review and revocation of their badge at any time based on consumer complaints or random re-examinations.

Over time, we could expect that businesses with the voluntary certification would attract more viewers. We might also expect these businesses to be able to command larger advertising placement fees. In short, we could use market-based mechanisms to encourage good behavior, improve the quality of information available, educate consumers about appropriate standards for truthfulness, and avoid the specter of censorship.

CHAPTER 17

Liking Something Can't Make It True

Originally published January 22, 2018.

One way to define something is to list the conditions or attributes that are necessary and sufficient for that thing to exist. The point of today's blog is to make a simple point about the definition of truth. Whether or not you like or agree with some statement is NEITHER necessary nor sufficient for that statement to be true.

Stated another way, we do not say that something is true merely because people approve of it. Rather, an assertion is true if and only if it can be shown that (1) the assertion corresponds to the world of experience or is coherent with the broader set of assertions that are known to be true, or both; and (2) the assertion could (at least in theory) be shown to be false through the existence of some (theoretically) identifiable outcomes or states of affairs.

You may like that, at sea level, water freezes at 32 degrees Fahrenheit. You may hate that water freezes at 32 degrees Fahrenheit. The fact that you like, or hate, the freezing point of water is completely irrelevant to the determination of whether it is true or false that water, at sea level, freezes at 32 degrees Fahrenheit. Truth is determined by whether water, at sea level, actually does turn into ice at 32 degrees Fahrenheit. How you or I feel about that just doesn't matter.

Consider the picture on the right. We can agree with others that the water in the glass on the left is frozen (it's not!), but that agreement will not and cannot make the water freeze. What makes water freeze are physical conditions independent of our likes, dislikes, agreements or disagreements. Specifically, physical conditions of temperature and pressure can change the density of water. The change to the density of water causes its volume to change, and this is what we observe when water changes to ice.

Water and Ice
Photo by Stephen Tryon

We can measure the temperature, pressure, density and volume of the water in the glass on the left. No matter how much your approval or disapproval changes, the fact of these changes to your approval or disapproval will not change the actual measurements of temperature, pressure, density and volume of the water in the glass. Another important way to characterize this situation is with the concept of falsifiability.

A statement is falsifiable when there are ways to confirm that it does NOT correspond to the world of shared experience. Consider the following statement A:

> The fact that you like, or hate, the freezing point of
> water is completely irrelevant to whether water freezes
> under given conditions of temperature and pressure.

Statement A is falsifiable because we can measure all the values and determine whether any changes to your approval or disapproval affect the temperature, pressure, density and volume of water. Statement A is true because there has never been an observation that satisfies its falsifiability conditions. We can say with full confidence that there never will be such an observation. If there ever is such an observation, we would have to change our assessment of Statement A from true to false.

By extension, the fact that you, or your neighbors, or the entire population of Kalamazoo, Michigan, LIKES something that some politician says has absolutely nothing to do with whether that politician's statement is true or false. Whether such a statement is true or false is determined by the set of necessary and sufficient conditions for truth that are expressed in the second paragraph of this essay. In this essay, we have used the concept of falsifiability to show that whether you like or dislike some assertion or state of affairs has absolutely nothing to do with that assertion or state of affairs being true or false.

CHAPTER 18

The Geometry of Truth

Originally published March 12, 2019.

Plato describes the wisdom of Socrates as knowing that he knew nothing at all. Rene Descartes' got around this skepticism about knowledge by noting that, even if all of our experience is a deceptive illusion, that illusion has to be presented to something. I remember how confused I was when I first read about Descartes, so I will present his reasoning once more here, using a slightly different approach.

Descartes said, "I am thinking, therefore I exist." In other words, even if all experience is an illusion, that illusion is like a movie, and there has to be something onto which the illusion is projected. We—each of us--are experiencing thought, and so we can be certain of one thing: our own existence as the thinker (Descartes 127).

Thus, we know we exist. We can use the fact of our existence and our natures as social animals to make a strong case for other truths. Once we depart from logical implications of conceptual knowledge, and begin to rely on our senses, things become less certain. We are confronted with experiences that we see, hear, touch, taste and smell. We can all agree that our individual perceptions of experience are imperfect. Those perceptions are sufficiently warped by emotion and bias in many cases to prevent agreement on the content and meaning of any given experience.

We need a standard for truth that we can apply together to help us make decisions. How can we leverage what we know to determine what is truth and what is illusion, to differentiate between facts and fake news? This essay provides part of the answer to that question by examining one of the necessary conditions for truth: that a proposition is true if it corresponds to the world of experience, or is coherent with the broader set of assertions that are known to be true, or both.

In a general sense, we can trace the concepts of correspondence and coherence to the differences between the philosophies of Plato and Aristotle. Plato was an idealist: he noted how imperfect our individual perceptions of experience can be, and concluded that reality must lie in a realm of pure Ideas. Aristotle was an empiricist: he accepted the imperfection of our perception of experience as part of what makes us human, and concluded that, for humans, reality had to be something we could infer from our observed experience.

Since Plato's Ideas (or Forms) are accessible only by reason, and the physical instances we encounter with our senses are only imperfect copies of Ideas, coherence works better as a model of truth in Plato's system. The measure of truth for a realm of rational Ideas is whether the ideas are logically consistent with one another. In other words, something is true if it fits with the set of all true things, which, for Plato, are Ideas.

Correspondence is a more intuitive measure of truth for Aristotle. Aristotle was an empiricist: he saw the physical world we experience through our senses as real and, when combined with our ability to reason, as our source of knowledge. Even if we see the physical world imperfectly, we have the ability to accumulate observations, think about those observations, and discern truth from them. For Aristotle, being able to verify a theory by its correspondence with our experience was necessary for truth.

But we should also note that correspondence and coherence should be complementary to one another because of what truth is, practically speaking. The principle of noncontradiction is one of the fundamental roots of reason: the principle states that it can never be the case that two logically contradictory states exist at the same time and place. If coherence and correspondence are not logically consistent, then one could imagine logically inconsistent things being true in a way that violates the principle of noncontradiction. Therefore, for our purpose of finding a yardstick for truth to use in social media and to measure the assertions made on the nightly news, we insist on being able to establish either correspondence or coherence, and we expect the two standards to be logically consistent.

This approach is consistent with the fact that the theories of both Plato and Aristotle emerged from a common intellectual root. The two men inherited their concepts of knowledge and truth from a tradition that went back at least 300 years to Pythagoras of Samos. The Pythagorean tradition was deeply rooted in mathematics as the purest form of knowledge. The Pythagorean Theorem remains a powerful example of a mathematical truth that corresponds with the empirical world and is coherent with the broader body of science.

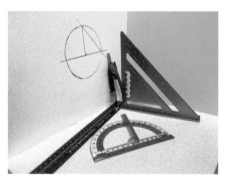

Photo by Stephen Tryon

Pythagoras had discovered a relationship between numbers based on the ancient set square, a tool used to true up the perpendiculars in the construction of temples and palaces for thousands of years. He had proven a universal relationship existed in the proportions of the lengths of the sides associated with the right triangle. Pythagoras demonstrated that the sum of the areas of squares constructed with the two shorter sides was always equal to the area of the square constructed using the hypotenuse.

The Pythagorean Theorem was the archetype of knowledge and truth. Here was a product of reason deeply tied to the world of experience and nature that we all share. Here was a fact consistent with every observation, from the crystalline structures of naturally occurring elements to the tools used to construct the pyramids. Here was a theorem revealing--through correspondence or coherence or both--eternal relationships in the structure of the universe that could be used to predict and build. By the time of Plato, Euclid had expanded on Pythagoras' work and published his system of geometry and geometric proofs (Bronowski).

A common modern definition of knowledge is "justified, true belief." There are three elements to this definition. To qualify as knowledge, a proposition has to be something in which we believe. Mere belief is a low bar. We all have beliefs. We disagree with each other about whose beliefs are better or more truthful. Knowledge must rely on something more.

Another element in our definition of knowledge is that it must be justified belief. That is somewhat better than belief alone--by adding the requirement for justification, we have to be able to offer reasonable grounds for our belief. But even this is not enough, as we can all offer reasons to believe things that are different from and inconsistent with what others have reason to believe.

There must be a stricter requirement to differentiate knowledge from belief, and that leads us to the requirement for truth. When we say that something qualifies as knowledge because it is justified *true* belief, the assertion of truth is a claim about the relationship between the proposition we are considering and the world of experience that we all share. We are asserting that the proposition corresponds with the world of experience or is coherent with the world of experience, or both, in the same way as the Pythagorean Theorem.

Things are not true because we want them to be true, or because someone we like tells us they are true, or even because we all agree that they are (or should be) true. Things are true if and only if it can be shown that (1) they correspond to the world of experience, or are coherent with the broader set of assertions that are known to be true, or both; and (2) they could (at least in theory) be shown to be false through the existence of some (theoretically) measurable outcomes or states of affairs. The essays in this section will continue our examination of these conditions for truth.

CHAPTER 19

Correspondence, Truth and Falsifiability

Originally published January 23, 2018.

In an earlier blog, we demonstrated that our personal feelings about some assertion--whether we like it or agree with it or not--are completely irrelevant to whether that assertion is true or false. Yet we hear our leaders on all sides condemn the views they do not like as "fake news." How can we determine whether news is true? What processes and standards should we use?

Two Views of the Hudson River Near West Point
Photo by Stephen Tryon

The first characteristic or attribute of the truth that comes to mind is that the truth corresponds with the real, physical world independent of our personal perspective. "Independent of our personal perspective" means that there is a way to confirm that what we, as individuals, think is "out there" *really is* out there. Ultimately, we want a test for truth that protects us from our cognitive bias.

The first method of confirmation that comes to mind is to ask other people to verify that what they see is the same as what we see. This type of confirmation is okay insofar as the testimony of other observers is trustworthy and reasonable, but there is a limit to what others' observations can confirm. The problem, of course, is that if we can be mistaken in our observations, others can be mistaken as well.

The picture appended to this post contains a photograph juxtaposed with a sketch of roughly the same view. The sketch (on the right) is of the Hudson River looking northward from Trophy Point at West Point, New York. The photograph on the left is an aerial view of the same general area of the Hudson River, taken from a point a few miles south of Trophy Point.

These pieces of art rest next to each other in my home. For me, they represent the correspondence dimension of truth--the correspondence of what our minds "see" with what is physically "there". Independent evidence that such a correspondence exists is evidence for the truth of a proposition or theory. Likewise, evidence that such a correspondence *does not* exist is evidence that a proposition or theory is false.

Using the observations of others to confirm a correspondence relationship is like asking others to draw their own sketches of the view from Trophy Point. It may confirm that all observers are seeing the same thing. It will probably also confirm that some of us are above average in artistic ability or eyesight. Multiple sketches may be better than relying on the perspective of a single observer, but still seem to fall short as a way of confirming what is causing our individual perceptions.

Applying the concept of falsifiability affords us a better solution. As you recall from our discussion of water freezing (Essay 17), a statement is falsifiable when there are ways to confirm that it *does not* correspond to the world of shared experience. We develop and test the falsifiability hypothesis in a particular situation by finding measurable variables that cause or are correlated with our observed experience.

In the case of our sketches from Trophy Point, our observed experience would seem to be a pattern of terrain features consisting of higher mountains on the left, a body of water dominating the center, and somewhat lower mountains on the right. We could measure the intensity and wavelength of the light coming to us from different angles. We could measure the time for light to travel from various parts of the scene to our position to establish the relative distance to each terrain feature. We could, in fact, build a matrix that captured values for all these variables at a given point in time. Given the lack of precision in our sketching process, perhaps we would need to rely on a range of values for each of the variables. Such a matrix could be our falsifiability condition: we could say that any depiction claiming to be the view from Trophy Point at the given point in time had to fit the ranges in our matrix in order to be "true."

Since the photograph to the left of the sketch above was not taken from Trophy Point, it would (appropriately) fail the falsifiability condition. However, if we were to take a picture with the same camera from the exact point and time from which the sketch was made, we could expect it to fit the ranges in our hypothetical matrix. The camera in question was not digital—it captured patterns of light by exposing chemically treated paper to the light as focused by the camera lens. We could construct a comparable matrix for a digital camera with pixels and the standards for portraying colors in electronic media.

The point of the preceding discussion is to show how falsifiability can be used to verify a correspondence relationship. Specifically, we determine the set of variables and values that we must match to establish correspondence. Then we apply the necessary instruments and measure the variables. Simple tests may be enough for simple states of affairs—we can verify whether a specific lamp in the dining room is on, for instance, by measuring the light present under that lamp.

What can we say about statements for which no falsifiability criteria are possible? It seems there are two cases. If the situation is that there are falsifiability criteria that simply cannot be measured due to technology limitations, then of course falsifiability criteria are theoretically possible, and we might consider using coherence in conjunction with those theoretical criteria in order to establish truth. If, on the other hand, there are no conceivable falsifiability conditions, theoretical or otherwise, then the statement in question can never be either true or false.

It seems then, that we have identified two attributes of truth that are necessary: (1) correspondence with the physical world outside of our individual perceptions, or the coherence of a single assertion with some broader set of true statements (or both correspondence and coherence); and (2) falsifiability – the possibility (at least in theory) of showing a proposition to be false through the existence of some (theoretically) identifiable variables and values. Theoretical falsifiability implies the ability to repeat processes that confirm truth criteria, and to predict that measurable variables and values will or will not occur during these iterations.

CHAPTER 20

Coherence, Truth and Falsifiability

Originally published January 24, 2018.

In previous essays, we have discussed two criteria that can be used to establish the truth or falsity of a proposition or theory. We also made the case that our personal feelings toward a proposition or theory--whether we like it or not--are irrelevant to whether that proposition or theory is true or false. In this essay, I review the criteria we discussed in prior blogs, with emphasis on the coherence dimension of truth.

Coherence: The Jigsaw Puzzle Model of Truth
Photo by Stephen Tryon

Here is a quick review of the criteria we have established as part of a checklist to determine whether something is true or false: (1) correspondence with the physical world outside of our individual perceptions, or the coherence of a theory or assertion with some broader set of true statements (or both correspondence and coherence); and (2) falsifiability – the possibility (at least in theory) of showing a proposition to be false through the existence of some (theoretically) identifiable variables and values. Theoretical falsifiability implies the ability to repeat processes that confirm truth criteria, and to predict that measurable variables and values will or will not occur during these iterations.

Evidence that a statement or assertion or theory is coherent with other facts, assertions, or theories supports the truth of the statement, assertion or theory under question. The phrase "is coherent with" means the assertion or theory under consideration, and all its antecedents and consequences, are logically consistent with the set of all other true statements and theories. At the most basic level, the claim that two statements are logically consistent with one another means that the two statements, together with all of their antecedents and consequences, don't lead to a contradiction.

We can illustrate the concept of logical contradiction with a simple example. Consider the following statements, A and B:

Statement A: A ball with a mass of 1kg, dropped from a platform 32 meters above the surface of the earth (at sea level, with no supplemental applied forces) will float upward like a balloon until it enters low earth orbit.

Statement B: Gravity exerts a force that pulls all objects towards the center of the earth with a force proportional to the mass of the earth and the distance between the earth and the object.

Statement A and Statement B are not logically consistent because the two statements lead us to a contradiction. Statement B, which we all know to be true, implies that the ball in Statement A must fall to the surface of the earth. Yet Statement A states that the ball floats upward until it enters low earth orbit. It cannot be the case that the ball both falls to the earth and floats upward like a balloon. Because the two statements generate a contradiction, we know one of them must be false.

Coherence tells us that Statement B is true. Statement B is consistent with our experience as well as with the laws of gravity as implied by Einstein's gravitational field equations. Those equations were experimentally tested and proven in 1919 when the sun's gravitational field was shown to bend light coming from a certain cluster of stars in the constellation Taurus (Isaacson 256-60). Statement B is logically consistent with gravity as an attractive force, and Statement A is not. Therefore, we can accept Statement B using coherence and falsifiability.

In the context of using coherence to establish truth, one falsifiability criterion (there may be others) is logical consistency. An assertion or theory is considered as ***not true*** when it leads to a contradiction with the set of all statements and theories that are true. This is different from how we applied the falsifiability criterion when we were using correspondence to establish truth (Essay 19).

By analogy, then, we can say that a proposition is true by coherence when the statement "fits" with other assertions, facts or theories that are commonly held to be true. The picture association with this essay--a jigsaw puzzle--is a great metaphor for coherence: we assemble jigsaw puzzles by determining where pieces fit. That process usually consists of some consideration of what the surrounding pieces look like: the pieces must be the correct shape, and the pattern on the pieces must blend appropriately to create the overall picture that is the subject of the puzzle.

CHAPTER 21

The Difference Between
Fact and Faith

Originally published January 15, 2019.

Faith can be a beautiful thing. An online dictionary defines faith as "complete trust or confidence in someone or something." In the context of religion, the same dictionary describes faith as "strong belief in God or in the doctrines of a religion, based on spiritual apprehension rather than proof" (google.com/'faith'). My personal faith is a great source of joy and comfort to me, but it is not fact, and I fear too many people do not understand the difference.

The First Amendment to the United States Constitution guarantees freedom of religion. That is a fact. The First Amendment was ratified on December 15, 1791 as part of the Bill of Rights. The text of the First Amendment states: "Congress shall make no law respecting an establishment of religion, or prohibiting the free exercise thereof..." ("The Constitution" 21). There is no debate about the text of the Amendment. These words were ratified by the several states and made part of the Constitution. The history of these words and the history of the ratification process, the product of a cooperative effort by many people in different state legislatures over a roughly contemporaneous period culminating in 1791, is irrefutable. There is no need for any leap beyond historical facts that everyone accepts.

On the contrary, the many different varieties of religious faith have sparked controversy, conflict and disagreement throughout history. The history of persecution of some religious groups by others was a principal motivation for the European migration to America, and subsequently, for the guarantee of freedom of religion in the United States Constitution. There is no framework of fact sufficient to establish the truth of any specific variety of religious belief. For that reason, a person who believes in any religion must go beyond what the facts can prove--they take a leap of faith.

Fact and Faith
Photo by Stephen Tryon

Under our Constitution, each person has the right to decide for themselves whether or not to take a "leap of faith." The choice a person makes--whether to believe or not believe something beyond what the facts can support--has no impact on their status as a citizen. The choice has no impact on the right of any person to equal protection of the laws.

But the constitutional protection of religious belief is not a blank check. We do not, for instance, allow the practice of human sacrifice, even though that practice has been part of some religions in the past. The reasoning is obvious--the Constitution guarantees equal protection of the law to all, and that is inconsistent with allowing religious practice that harms non-believers.

For their part, non-believers sometimes act as if their reliance on facts--and by facts, I mean those statements whose truth can be verified independently using tests such as correspondence, coherence, and falsifiability—makes them more worthy than believers. Facts definitely have more utility than faith in the realms of science, engineering, criminal justice and similar professions. However, the constitutional guarantee of equal protection of the laws applies equally to people acting on the basis of religious faith as well as to those acting on the basis of fact.

There is a bit of natural tension between religious faith and fact, but the two are not mutually exclusive because there are significant limits to what we know. Most of the matter and energy in the universe are "dark", and do not interact with light or other matter the same as ordinary matter and energy--we don't know what this stuff is! (Tyson 59-60, 108-140). Keeping what we can know to be true in perspective leaves room for reasonable people to choose faith, or not, and to tolerate those whose faith choice is different from their own. Indeed, even scientists can (and do) choose to take the leap of faith in realms they know are not governed by fact.

The limits of factual knowledge leave plenty of room for faith, but not the overly specific faith that most religions espouse. There is a clear factual record that supports the current theory for the evolution of life on earth from the Big Bang to homo sapiens. But in the words of astrophysicist Neil Degrasse Tyson, "What happened before the beginning? [We] have no idea..... religious people assert... that something must have started it all.... In the mind of such a person, that something is, of course, God" (Tyson 32). The factual record leaves room for belief in God. It doesn't support the culturally-driven, anthropomorphic mythologies we generally associate with organized religion. And it definitely doesn't support persecuting one another over the differences between our various mythologies. In other words, the factual record demands tolerance of differences in religious faith--because of all we don't know--it supports the First Amendment.

CHAPTER 22

Ockham's Razor and the Deep State Conspiracy Theory

Originally published April 8, 2018.

William of Ockham was a 14th-century Christian cleric and philosopher. He is famous for formulating a "rule of thumb" that is known as Ockham's Razor. The rule is simply this: if you have to choose between theories, you should choose the theory that relies on the fewest assumptions. That seems like common sense. Assumptions are substitutes for facts--our best guesses that we use to fill in the blanks where we don't have facts. It seems pretty reasonable to say that the theory with the most facts and the fewest assumptions, wins.

That is especially true when you consider that, if you are willing to make enough assumptions, you can choose to believe just about anything. And your belief will be "unfalsifiable". Because as soon as anyone presents you with evidence that your belief is false, you will simply introduce another assumption--an ad hoc hypothesis--to explain away the evidence that has been presented.

Let us consider the many recent conspiracy theories about the Justice Department and the intelligence community. Robert Mueller's investigation produced over 30 indictments, including 13 Russians accused of espionage. These indictments are approved by a grand jury. A grand jury is 16 to 23 Americans chosen for jury duty in the same manner jurors are chosen in your hometown. And on a grand jury, 3/4 of the total number of jurors must approve an indictment before it is handed down (Mueller 174-99).

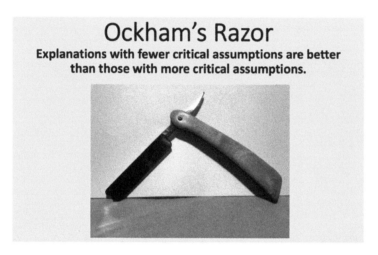

Graphic and Photo by Stephen Tryon

Mueller's investigation also produced several guilty pleas from Americans who worked on the Trump campaign or transition team. These people confessed to lying about their contacts with Russians. Some were sentenced to serve time in jail for perjury and other crimes. In response to this, even though the Special Counsel is a Republican, conservatives assert that the American justice department and intelligence community are engaged in a politically motivated conspiracy to attack and undermine President Trump.

Contrast the results of Mueller's investigation with the many investigations that occurred in the Obama administration. There was a steady stream of investigations, including the Special Committee on Benghazi, which holds the record for the longest congressional investigation in our history. Yet those investigations did not produce a single indictment or guilty plea. And even in the fifteen months since the Republicans have gained control of the Executive Branch, there are no charges, no indictments, no guilty pleas.

We are confronted with two hypotheses. On the one hand, we can accept the facts at face value. Assuming that the system of procedural justice has been applied uniformly in both cases, the difference in outcomes is a reflection of real wrongdoing on the part of the Trump campaign and transition team and the absence of wrongdoing on the part of the Obama administration.

On the other hand, we can start adding "ad hoc hypotheses" to explain why there are tangible results from the current Special Counsel's investigation and no tangible results from the many investigations during the Obama administration. We can assume that Republicans and Democrats in the Justice and intelligence communities conspired to protect President Obama and Hillary Clinton several years before Donald Trump decided to run for President. Oh yeah, and all of the press except Fox News was in on it, too.

We can further assume that these diverse conspirators also decided to attack and undermine an administration of the opposite party once Trump was elected. These are all ad hoc hypotheses. If there was evidence of a "deep state" conspiracy, the Republican Attorney General could have produced his own indictments. He did not do so.

I know what William of Ockham would say!

CHAPTER 23

A Simple Example of Fake News

Originally published May 1, 2018.

Dear President Trump: You constantly call news reports you do not like "fake news." That is not correct. Whether you like something or not doesn't make it fake news. What makes a news report "fake news" is when it fails the time-tested standards for truth. For instance, when the reported event does not correspond to the world of shared experience which we all inhabit together, that is fake news. But just in case that definition is a bit too much for you, let me show you a clear example of fake news, and explain why it is fake news.

The headline circled in the picture accompanying this essay, and the story to which it refers, is fake news ("Trump Passed Polygraph" 1). The headline is fake news because it isn't true. You see, a polygraph refers to a specific type of machine and process for determining whether someone is telling the truth. I could cite lots of definitions from well-respected sources giving basically the same definition, but I will just give one. The Legal Dictionary defines the process and equipment as follows:

> ...a trained examiner fits a subject with sensors to measure
> respiration, heart rate and blood pressure, and perspiration,

which the polygraph records using pens on graph paper. The examiner asks a series of questions, including control questions that are designed to provoke anxiety and denial. Later, another examiner compares these answers with answers pertaining to the matter at hand.

That is what a polygraph is.

But when you read the article, you discover that it doesn't really say you took a polygraph. Instead, using a machine called a Voice Stress Analyzer, somebody I've never heard of says they can analyze your voice remotely and determine your stress level and tell whether you are telling the truth. There are at least two major problems with this claim. First, the National Research Council, after studying all the available literature on the Voice Stress Analyzer technology, said "this research and the few controlled tests conducted over the past decade offer little or no scientific basis for the use of the computer voice stress analyzer or similar voice measurement instruments" (NAP 12-13, 166-168). In other words, there is no evidence that the technology cited by the National Enquirer works the way a polygraph works. Second, since you never were fitted with sensors to measure your respiration, heart rate, blood pressure, and perspiration while being asked both control and truth-test questions, you never took a polygraph. Therefore, since the headline asserts that you passed a polygraph, when in fact you have not, it is fake news.

An Example of Fake News
Photo by Stephen Tryon

What was NOT fake news was the Special Counsel's investigation. The information generated by that investigation was vetted and assessed by a grand jury of 16 to23 American citizens chosen at random, just like every other jury in America. That grand jury resulted in more than 30 indictments, convictions and guilty pleas. Over 20 of the people indicted were Russian nationals, and they were indicted for interfering with the 2016 presidential election. Of the remaining indictments, five of the people indicted pleaded guilty to lying to investigators about their contacts with Russian officials during your campaign and transition. It is obvious that those outcomes are NOT fake news. A whole bunch of American citizens have looked at a ton of evidence and have produced indictments and guilty pleas and even jail sentences. The Special Counsel's investigation is tied to the world we all inhabit together in some very tangible, measurable ways (Mueller 9-10, 174-99).

I hope this little primer helps you use the term "fake news" correctly in the future. But I'm not holding my breath.

CHAPTER 24

Fake News and Donald Trump's Big Lie

Originally published June 20, 2021.

The idea that we are now talking about our 45th Commander-in-Chief in terms of his "big lie" is troubling. After all, according to the Washington Post, Donald Trump lied to or misled the American people 30,573 times during his four years in office (Kessler, et. al.). While a president who lies so brazenly bothers me a great deal, what is even more troubling is the fact that so many elected and appointed officials continue to support this unworthy character in his pursuit of Government-By-Criminal-Enterprise, and that so many voters seem willing to tolerate the cabal.

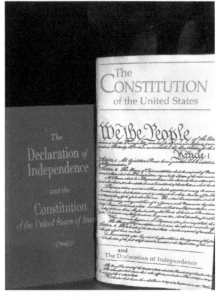

Principles and Processes
Photo by Stephen Tryon

We have apparently lost the ability to judge the character of our public officials, and to hold our elected and appointed officials accountable to the high standards we should demand from public servants. All our Memorial Day, Flag Day, and Independence Day platitudes are meaningless if we, collectively, are not willing to hold public officials accountable for being honest stewards of the values so many have paid the ultimate price to preserve.

In this essay, I want to review the facts around Trump's big lie. Specifically, I will consider these facts in light of my prior essays about fake news and how to tell whether something is true or false. It is clear from all available evidence that Trump's assertions about election fraud are false: they fail every reasonable test for truth-by-correspondence, truth-by-coherence, and falsifiability.

Trump's attempt to overturn the constitutionally proper election of Joe Biden as the 46th President of the United States reflects a disgusting unwillingness to acknowledge the will of the American people. Biden's victory was not at all a surprise. Every credible news source reported Biden far ahead of Trump in nationwide polling during the weeks and months preceding election day. Trump never had a chance to win the popular vote. He could have been elected if he had won enough electoral college votes, but he clearly did not win either the popular vote or the electoral college.

Trump's response to his bad poll performance was predictable: he claimed it was fake news and that the only way he could lose was if the election was rigged. In fact, there was no surprise in the general election results nationally: Biden was ahead of Trump by a significant margin before the election, and Biden won the election by seven million votes. The only surprise was that Trump persisted in a transparent attempt to deceive his supporters into believing there was some irregularity in the results, and the fact that so many of his supporters believed his lies in spite of overwhelming evidence to the contrary.

Trump's pre-election propaganda alleged there was a plot to steal the election through widespread fraud in mail-in ballots and voting machine irregularities in districts with large populations of minority voters.

Because of his allegations that mail-in voting was somehow more fraudulent than voting in person, most news sources predicted Trump's supporters would vote in person and avoid voting by mail. Thus, experts expected the same day vote to skew in Trump's favor while the mail-in and early voting would favor Biden. Although this was completely expected, and it was known that the mail-in ballots would not be counted until after the in-person vote in many cases, Trump and his campaign messaged that any late shift in Biden's favor was somehow evidence of fraud. In short, Trump made false claims that voting expected to go against him was somehow fraudulent, and that the totally predictable and normal pattern of vote counting was somehow evidence that supported his false claims.

After losing the election, the president used every available tool to spread his big lie that the election was stolen and to seek to overturn the results. His campaign demanded multiple recounts in key states. He had the Attorney General launch an investigation using Justice Department assets. Trump and his allies launched over 50 lawsuits against election processes and officials in key states. Trump himself directly pressured elected and appointed officials at state and local level to fraudulently change election results. He invited election officials from Michigan to the White House to pressure them into refusing to certify the election results in that state. In a recorded phone call, we hear him begging Georgia Secretary of State Brad Raffensperger (a Republican) to find him the 11,780 votes he needed to reverse Biden's victory in Georgia ("Trump begs Georgia secretary of state...").

Trump's relentless attempts to make his claims of election fraud stick in the minds of his supporters eventually led to the January 6th insurrection on Capitol Hill, and caused major social media outlets to ban him from posting on the basis that his posts constituted misinformation. In spite of Trump's unprecedented attempts to delegitimize the 2020 election, it was clear at every step that his claims failed to satisfy the basic requirements for truth. Trump's allegations of fraud are not true by correspondence, and they are not true by coherence.

Trump's allegations of fraud fail the test of truth by correspondence because the many attempts to recount, or sue, or investigate fraud led to local, state and federal officials and judges of both political parties finding that the original election results were accurate, that Trump's team had insufficient evidence to justify their lawsuits, and that federal investigations showed no meaningful problems with the conduct of the election. With regard to the Dominion voting machine conspiracy, the Department of Homeland Security's Cybersecurity & Infrastructure Security Agency immediately refuted Trump's claims ("Election Security Rumor Vs. Reality"). With regard to Trump's allegations of fraud in general, his own Attorney General declared that investigations by U.S. Attorneys and FBI agents "have not seen fraud on a scale that could have effected a different outcome in the election" (apnews.com). Election officials across the country followed normal procedures to certify Biden's victory. Numerous recounts validated the results. Tens of lawsuits and legal maneuvers alleging voter fraud were denied or dismissed. In Pennsylvania, for instance, Republican judge Matthew Brann ruled that Trump's legal team presented "strained legal arguments without merit and speculative accusations ... unsupported by evidence" ("...Federal judge eviscerates Trump lawsuit"). If Trump's claims were true, then there would have been some pattern of credible election officials, judges or federal investigators substantiating those claims in the immediate aftermath of the election. There was no such pattern. Therefore, we conclude the claims were false.

Trump's allegations of fraud fail the test of truth by coherence because the kinds of facts that would emerge, in some form, across the more than 3,100 distinct jurisdictions with election responsibilities were denied by every credible investigation, review and recount of the election. Officials of both parties play a role in each of the more than 3,100 jurisdictions that administer a federal general election. Carrying out a conspiracy and fraud on the scale suggested by Trump's claims would be very difficult because it would have to involve a lot of different people, including some with differing political alignments. Carrying out such a plot without leaving any evidence of the plot is inconceivable.

By January of 2017, less than 2 months after Trump won the 2016 general election, the CIA, DIA and FBI had detected a pattern of events—fake social media profiles, for instance—that they were able to assess as part of a Russian conspiracy to impact the 2016 general election. In a joint statement released on January 6, 2017, the three agencies went on the record with the following statement:

> Russian efforts to influence the 2016 US presidential
> election... demonstrated a significant escalation in
> directness, level of activity and scope of effort compared
> to previous operations... We further assess Putin and the
> Russian Government developed a clear preference
> for President-elect Trump. We have high confidence in
> these judgments (dni.gov).

In a completely separate and independent investigation, Republican Special Counsel Robert Mueller confirmed the assessment of the intelligence community, and secured enough evidence to produce over 30 indictments (including Russian government officials), several guilty pleas, and jail time for some members of Trump's campaign. Mueller's report states that

> As set forth in detail in this report, the Special Counsel's
> investigation established that Russia interfered in the
> 2016 presidential election principally through two oper-
> ations. First, a Russian entity carried out a social media
> campaign that favored presidential candidate Donald J.
> Trump and disparaged presidential candidate Hillary
> Clinton. Second, a Russian intelligence service con-
> ducted computer-intrusion operations against entities,
> employees, and volunteers working on the Clinton
> Campaign and then released stolen documents. The
> investigation also identified numerous links between
> the Russian government and the Trump Campaign.

> Although the investigation established that the Russian
> government perceived it would benefit from a Trump
> presidency and worked to secure that outcome, and that
> the Campaign expected it would benefit electorally from
> information stolen and released through Russian efforts,
> the investigation did not establish that members of the
> Trump Campaign conspired or coordinated with the
> Russian government in its election interference activi-
> ties (justice.gov/archives).

It would be difficult to carry out fraud such as that which Trump claims cost him the 2020 election. It would be virtually impossible to do so without leaving a pattern of evidence such as that discovered within 2 months of the 2016 election.

If the massive fraud Trump alleges took place, there would be a pattern of evidence consistent with that fraud, much as there was in the wake of the 2016 election. As determined by Trump's own Attorney General and many others, there simply is no pattern of facts consistent with the kind of conspiracy Trump claims to have occurred. Therefore, Trump's claims of election fraud fail the test of truth by coherence.

Many Trump supporters believe his claims as an article of faith. Therefore, although there are falsifiability criteria for Trump's claims, and those criteria have been met and confirmed by numerous independent authorities from both parties, many Trump supporters simply throw out another ad-hoc conspiracy hypothesis as a rebuttal. Their refusal to accept any reasonable falsifiability criteria makes their continued claims of fraud logically meaningless (albeit dangerous to the integrity of our republic).

The ongoing efforts by Trump and his allies to continue the audits of the 2020 election prove without a doubt that Trump's claims of election fraud are not merely false—they are nothing less than a low-intensity insurrection. The audits are simply a ploy to delegitimize a perfectly legitimate American election by creating an endless source of ad hoc conspiracy hypotheses. Trump's claims are political nihilism—nothing less than a cynical embrace of might-makes-right politics and the complete abnegation of his oath to support the United States Constitution and the rule of law.

Study Questions and Key Terms

STUDY QUESTIONS

1. Explain the line of reasoning Descartes uses to prove knowledge is possible. Write the premises and conclusion in the form of a deductive argument.

2. Essay 20 defines how a proposition may be shown to be true by coherence and falsifiability. Write out a deductive argument that you think best represents the author's reasoning in this essay.

3. Are there different kinds of facts? Describe and discuss how the three conditions of knowledge discussed in this section—justified true belief—apply to historical facts, scientific facts, and demographic facts.

4. Essay 21 makes an argument that both the choice to believe in a religious intuition as well as the choice to not believe in a religious intuition are both reasonable choices. Write out a deductive argument that you think best represents the author's reasoning in this essay.

5. Explain how Ockham's Razor supports falsifiability as a criterion for truth.

KEY TERMS

1. Descartes - a French philosopher, soldier, mathematician, and scientist, famous for his proof of the possibility of knowledge. He lived in the first half of the 17th century (1596-1650).

2. necessary condition – a condition or set of condition whose satisfaction partially establishes the presence of a given state.

3. sufficient condition – a condition or set of conditions whose satisfaction fully establishes the presence of a given state.

4. correspondence - the existence of a relationship between a descriptor and the state of affairs it describes in reality such that the state of affairs is repeatable, predictable, and falsifiable.

5. coherence - logical agreement between a state of affairs and the set of other propositions known to be true.

6. Pythagoras – Greek philosopher who demonstrated that the sum of the areas of squares formed by the shorter sides of any right triangle always equal the area of the square formed by the longest side of that triangle. Because this relationship is repeatable, predictable and verifiable, it is a good example of the correspondence attribute of truth.

7. verifiable- able to be confirmed;

8. repeatable – characteristic of a process enabling the process to be consistently performed and to produce a predictable outcome; characteristic of a state of affairs such that it can be recreated in a consistent fashion.

9. predictable – characteristic of a process or outcome such that it can be accurately described before the process is run or the outcome is produced.

10. logical consequence – an outcome or state of affairs that can be reasonably predicted to occur based on a preceding set of conditions

11. faith - the belief or confidence in someone or something based on intuition rather than factual proof

12. Ockham's Razor – a rule of thumb holding that, among competing theories, the one that relies on the fewest assumptions or ad hoc hypotheses is the most likely to be true.

13. ad hoc hypothesis - something that must be invented or assumed in order to defend the truth of a theory or assertion.

14. conspiracy theory – proposal that some (often negative) outcome was the result of a premeditated and coordinated plot

15. deduction and induction - two distinct methods of reasoning to a logical consequence from a preceding assertion; with deduction, the content or denotation of one or more concepts is shown to imply a certain conclusion based on patterns of rational relationships; with induction, a pattern of observed events is combined with patterns of rational relationships to imply a likely conclusion (acknowledging epistemic uncertainty).

PART V

Changes We Need

Bottom Line Up Front

The main idea of this section is to suggest ways to increase accountability of our federal government. The flood of information unleashed by information-age technology has overwhelmed our capacity to hold government accountable. We need to educate our citizens and modify our institutions to accomplish the six purposes of the federal government (Ch 25). Congressional information systems should better engage and inform citizens (Ch 26). We must incorporate state-of-the-art information security mechanisms and audit capability to protect these systems (Ch 27). We should improve electoral processes for all registered voters with legislation like the Open Our Democracy Act (Ch 28). We should shift the basis on which we draw boundaries for all legislative districts to minimize the number of disenfranchised voters (Ch 29). Finally, we should choose representatives based on demonstrated character and public service (Ch 30).

CHAPTER 25

Time, Space, Population and the Purposes of Government

Originally published August 15, 2019.

"We the People of the United States, in Order to form a more perfect Union, establish Justice, insure domestic Tranquility, provide for the common defense, promote the general Welfare, and secure the Blessings of Liberty to ourselves and our Posterity, do ordain and establish this Constitution for the United States of America." These are the six purposes for the government as they are listed at the beginning of the Constitution of the United States. There may be differences of opinion about how the government should pursue these purposes, but there can be no doubt that these are the words given in the Constitution to define the general scope of the government's authority.

On closer examination, we can probably agree on more than just the list of general purposes. We can probably agree that a government charged with establishing justice, ensuring domestic tranquility and promoting the general welfare of 1000 people has a more difficult task than a government charged with the same responsibilities for a population of 100 people. These tasks, in particular, and perhaps the others as well, are pretty clearly tasks that require a bigger government for a larger population than for a smaller population. These three purposes of our government, at least, involve mediating the interactions between citizens, especially when those interactions involve conflict. As the number of people in a society increases, or more accurately, as the *effective population density* increases, we might expect the number of interactions requiring government mediation to increase as well. We can use effective population density as a yardstick to approximate, at least on a relative basis, how much government is required to achieve the purposes identified by our Constitution.

Effective population density captures the idea that, as you increase the number of people in a given area, and increase the technology with which they can affect the people around them, you will increase the number of interactions that are likely to require government regulation or intervention. Basically, if the Hatfields and McCoys want to go off in the middle of nowhere and have a feud that doesn't affect anyone around them, some might say that is their business. But move that feud to downtown Manhattan at rush hour, and we can probably agree that the government has an interest--a duty even--to intervene, mediate, regulate, control or prevent the feud. To properly "establish Justice, insure domestic Tranquility,... [and] promote the general Welfare" of all the innocent bystanders who would be hurt by the fight in downtown Manhattan, we can probably all agree the government has a duty under our Constitution to intervene.

In the era of the founding of the United States of America (1775-1788) it took 7-10 days to travel the 308 miles from Lexington and Concord to Philadelphia, depending on whether you rode a horse or rode in a carriage. Let's take the low end of that range: 7 days is 168 hours. So the speed of information was roughly 2 mph. There were about 3 million colonists and slaves living in the original states, which controlled at most an area of about 200,000 square miles, for an average population density of roughly 15 people per square mile. We might assign a "technology factor" to account for the fact that, in a given space, the ability of one person to affect or communicate with other people was limited by the range of their voice, or, if they were fortunate enough to know how to read and write, by their access to a book or newspaper. Even the effective range of common weapons was limited to a fraction of a mile, and their rate of fire, for an expert, was 2 to 3 rounds per minute. But there were newspapers, and according to the census of 1790 we can estimate that about 5 percent of the population lived in cities. So let's arbitrarily assign a technology factor of 5. Given all this, then, we might calculate the effective population density to be 2 miles per hour times 15 people per square mile times a technology factor of 5 for an effective population density of about 150.

Today, in the United States, we have about 330 million people living on 3.8 million square miles, or roughly 87 people per square mile. Today, information travels at the speed of light: roughly 671 million mph. Multiplying those numbers together, even with the simplifying assumption that the technology factor is part of the increase in the speed of information, yields a staggering 58 trillion. On this view, the effective population density of the United States today is nearly 400 million times what it was in 1790.

This number is probably way too big. After all, the combined speed-of-information-and-technology factor in the second calculation masks the fact that the significance of many individual transactions has also lessened as the cost of communicating with each other has gone down and the frequency has gone up. Not every email can be equated to a Hatfield-McCoy feud in its impact on justice, domestic tranquility, and the general welfare. But even with other reasonable, if arbitrary, reductions, the fact remains that modern society is exponentially more complex than the society the framers of our Constitution experienced.

The quality and quantity of changes between their society and ours are so great that the men who wrote and ratified the Constitution could not have imagined all the things that would be necessary today to achieve the purposes they enumerated for our government. They could not have imagined, for instance, e-commerce and air traffic safety and cybercrime. But they gave us the six purposes they thought any government of free people should aim to accomplish: "to form a more perfect

Union, establish Justice, insure domestic Tranquility, provide for the common defense, promote the general Welfare, and secure the Blessings of Liberty to ourselves and our Posterity." As I see it, that all basically boils down to regulating interactions between people within our society and with people in other countries in such a way as to keep us all from having to go to war with each other to secure our basic rights.

People who complain that government is too big or is too involved in our daily lives should offer a blueprint for how, exactly, government is supposed to "form a more perfect Union, establish Justice, insure domestic Tranquility, provide for the common defense, promote the general Welfare, and secure the Blessings of Liberty to ourselves and our Posterity" in today's society *without* being more involved in our daily lives than it was in the days before electricity. If the purposes of government are to regulate interactions between people to remove the need for those people to resort to the Hatfield-and-McCoy type of solution, then I think the government should be big enough to accomplish that purpose. And I think that, when it comes time to elect people to serve in our government, or to decide whether to support some new idea, we should consider our choices in the context of the purposes of government as identified in our Constitution.

The power of this approach is that it provides a simple, shared framework for discussion and argument that is independent of your political party, your religion, or the color of your skin. Using the framework will not answer every question or solve all of our disagreements, but it will allow us to focus on whether or not some proposed law is a legitimate exercise of governmental power. Because frankly, there is nothing in the Constitution that says I have to agree with your ideas on religion, or your political philosophy, or your ideas on how to improve society. In fact, the Constitution gives me the express right to disagree with you and everyone else on all of those things. We are more likely to achieve meaningful outcomes if we use the framework provided in the Constitution to focus our discussions about what government should do on any single issue than if we waste time on matters where we are all entitled to our own opinion.

The beauty and power of the United States Constitution is not that it contains a tailor-made solution for every new type of problem that has emerged over the past 230 years. Rather, the beauty of our Constitution is that it contains a framework for tapping the wisdom of each generation to solve that generation's problems. The beauty of the Constitution is that it recognizes one thing does not change--people continue to disagree over how to use the resources of our society to solve the problems we face. The beauty of our Constitution is that it includes fair processes for considering opposing viewpoints as we try to resolve our disagreements. The proper use of our Constitution is not to suppress dissent or to take us backwards to some imagined "good old days." The magic of our Constitution is its power to use reason to leverage our differences, with all parties making the best possible case for how their programs, proposals and candidates can help us "form a more perfect Union, establish Justice, insure domestic Tranquility, provide for the common defense, promote the general Welfare, and secure the Blessings of Liberty to ourselves and our Posterity".

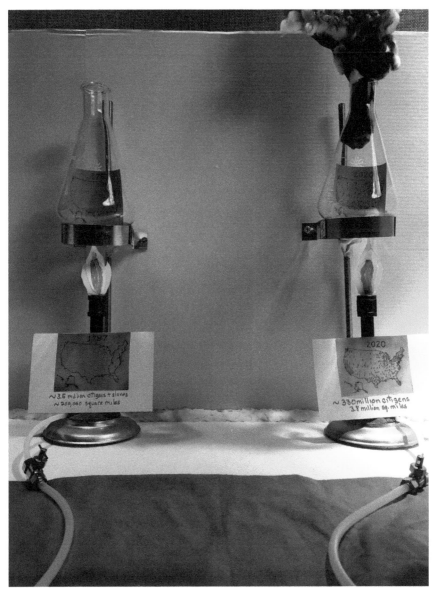

American Experiment 1787 and 2020
Photo by Stephen Tryon

CHAPTER 26

Technology and Government

Originally published December 19, 2019.

One of the major premises of *Accountability Citizenship* is that, over the past 50 years or so, technology has changed what it takes to be a good citizen of the democratic republic that we call the United States of America. Technology unleashed the crushing flood of information in which we are all immersed. Technology enabled the increasingly accurate personalization of this flood of information to surround each of us with a bubble tailor-made to convince us that we know, as individuals, what is right and best and true (and to make it very easy to buy things related to our basic needs and world view). Technology allows us to choose channels and form groups that reinforce our individual world view while, in many cases, objectifying and demonizing those who have a different world view. Technology has, in many ways, made it more difficult to form consensus, to build solutions that reflect compromise, and even to recognize that compromise is necessary.

Being a good citizen requires that we try to understand the world we inhabit, that we share our understanding with others in a manner respectful of those with a different understanding, and that we work together to implement effective solutions to the many challenges that confront us. Technology has caused or intensified many of the challenges we face. But technology is also absolutely necessary to building and implementing effective solutions to those challenges. Technology can enable systems that allow us to inform our (and our fellow citizens') understanding of major challenges facing our society, to consolidate and summarize individual perspectives on possible responses to those challenges, and to protect the integrity and availability of the information associated with challenges, solutions, and citizen inputs.

Technology is Indispensable for Effective Governance.
Photo by Stephen Tryon

In the first edition of *Accountability Citizenship*, I introduced the idea of using technology on the web site of every Member of Congress to create something I called Congress 2.0. The basic idea was to convert the web site of every Member of Congress from the one-way information bulletin boards that they are today into secure, comprehensive, two-way platforms for anonymously collecting and displaying the sentiments and priorities of every registered voter in every congressional district. Along with the survey tool, a Congress 2.0 web site would incorporate a dynamic scorecard mechanism that would display the performance of each district's Member of Congress as measured by the priorities of registered voters in the district and performance metrics common to all Members of Congress (like attendance and percentage of missed votes).

There were a few illustrations in the first book to give readers the general idea of what the tool would do. Unfortunately, no Member of Congress accepted my challenge to incorporate such technology into their web site. My own congressional delegation offered nonsensical reasons why they "cannot" (really, should be "will not") add this technology to their taxpayer-funded web sites.

Over the course of the past six years, as I have pursued degrees in computer science and information systems, my understanding of the technology has increased to the point where I built a "mockup" of the Congress 2.0 web site, or, as I now call it, the Voter Transparency Tool (VTT). The technology to build and secure the VTT has also improved dramatically. In this blog, I include a few screenshots to show how the voter logs in, records their input, and checks the current VTT survey results for their district and state. For those interested in testing the working mockup, you will be able to access that on accountabilitycitizenship.org soon.

The login functionality is just the same as we are all used to for logging in to our online bank accounts. Your voter registration number serves as both your user id and account number. When you log in for the first time, you create a password long enough to provide reasonable security. For additional security, multi-factor authentication is mandatory. That means you have to use your fingerprint or respond to a system-generated message on another device you own or another secure web site in order to gain access to the survey and see statewide results for your state. The initial login page is shown here:

Voter Transparency Tool Log in
Mockup by Stephen Tryon

Once the voter logs in, they are redirected to the survey page. The survey shown in the mockup includes a question about abortion, a question about budget discipline, a question about the re-districting process for elected officials, and a space for voters to nominate issues they want to see included in future revisions of the Voter Transparency Tool survey. While

much of the data could be the same in all congressional districts in a state, it is important to build the tool from the level of the congressional district to enable registered voters in each district to nominate the issues they feel are most important. So in each state, the VTT for the two senators will be identical, but there could be different survey questions in the VTT for each Member of the House of Representative's congressional district. Here is what the mockup survey page looks like:

When the voter completes their responses to the survey questions, and clicks on the submit button, they are taken to the results page. The results page provides a receipt of the individual input recorded for that particular voter, and it also provides a graphical summary view of the counts of registered voters in each county in the state who have voted on the same issues. In the mockup itself, voters will be able to click on the summary data for each county to see an expanded view of the numbers of voters who have recorded survey votes in favor of the issue and opposed to the issue, as well as a tally of those who have not voted. You can find a representation of how the survey results might appear at the end of this essay.

The Voter Transparency Tool would accomplish a number of beneficial effects in our country. First, it would make voter participation fun and would give people a reason to register. No one would want to be the person who could not log in to the VTT; most people would be curious about what issues their fellow citizens nominated as the most important, as well as how people in various counties voted on specific issues. The tool would also display a dynamic scorecard (not shown here) on the senators and the representative associated with each district. Members of Congress would have an incentive to manage their score, and that would require much more extensive engagement with their constituents than is currently the case.

There is no doubt that a major increase in the quantity and quality of available information has radically changed the requirements for effective citizenship in the United States over the past fifty years. In my view, we as a society have failed to provide the education and the information management tools to enable healthy citizenship in this new environment. Our failure has created a vacuum that has been filled by special interests. Those interests are now manipulating the information stream to further their own agendas; this has the second-order effects of discouraging participation, increasing polarization, and degrading our ability to identify and solve the most pressing challenges we face. The Voter Transparency Tool is one way we can use information technology to enable efficient management and accountability for our republic.

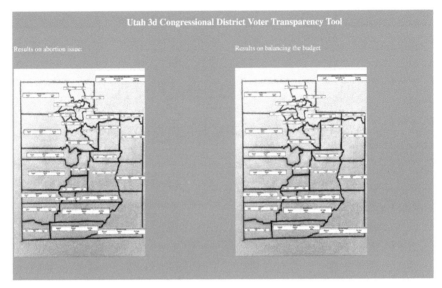

Representation of Voter Transparency Tool Survey Results
Mockup by Stephen Tryon

CHAPTER 27

Election System Security
and Blockchain

Originally published January 10, 2020.

First, let's be perfectly clear--any information system can be hacked if enough resources are available to attack it. Given that fact, the only attainable objectives when securing an information system are (1) to make the time and resources required to break the system greater than than the value gained by breaking the system, and (2) to make any breach visible to the system's owners. In the context of electoral processes in general, the potential "value" of the attack could be to demonstrate the capability to disrupt an election in order to extract ransom from an unprepared government. Alternatively, the motive could be political rather than monetary, and the value in this case would be to undermine faith in the electoral process, to deny a government the ability to declare a valid outcome, or to change the outcome without anyone in the target country being aware of the hack.

Protecting the validity of election outcomes is, of course, fundamental to the viability of a republic such as the United States. Famous rulings by the Supreme Court in the 1960s established that equal protection of the law, guaranteed to each citizen under the Fourteenth Amendment, applied to the individual's right to vote. In *Baker v. Carr*, the Court ruled that the Tennessee legislature had to redistrict based on population, with the intention of ensuring that everyone's vote counted equally. Attacks on electoral systems that favor one party over another, besides being *prima facie* illegal, threaten this principle of equal protection of the law. Protecting electoral processes that provide a valid outcome wherein each registered voter can be certain their vote was not tampered with or discarded is therefore essential to protecting the right to vote.

Photo by Stephen Tryon

Proper information security protects the confidentiality, integrity and availability (C-I-A) of the information in an information system. Safeguarding confidentiality means we keep secret things secret, allowing only authorized people to see data that has been restricted from public view in some way. Protecting the integrity of information means keeping the data safe from changes caused by any unauthorized person or process. Ensuring availability means that all authorized users can access the systems and information they need at designated times and places without interruption. In a well-designed system, information security professionals use a layered approach of physical and procedural safeguards in conjunction with dedicated hardware and software resources to detect and defend against attacks.

This traditional layered approach is the best defense against attacks aimed at the confidentiality and availability dimensions of an electoral information system. While voting machines, by definition, must be accessible to the public, the physical security of these machines should include inspection and certification that each machine functions properly and has not been tampered with prior to election day. From the point of certification, election officials must ensure proper chain of custody and protection from unauthorized access to the machines until the polls open. During the election, proper access control ensures only registered voters touch the machines and only for the purpose of casting their individual vote. Other nodes in the electoral system should be protected with the same physical security measures used to protect sensitive data centers--access only by authorized people with appropriate credentials for specific, official purposes. Information must be encrypted at rest and in transit, with hardware and software firewalls along with appropriately hardened network infrastructure protecting access to the transmissions and storage locations for the encrypted data. Technology staff access should be segmented, monitored, and guarded by appropriately complex multi-factor authentication and authorization protocols.

Traditional defenses remain important for the integrity of information in information systems. So-called ransomware attacks modify data in an information system by encrypting it, compromising the integrity of the data in a way that denies availability of the system to authorized users until some sum of money is paid to the attackers. To protect against this type of attack, systems must not only prevent unauthorized access, but also must ensure that authorized inputs to systems and software are validated to screen out malicious code that could alter system data.

For electoral systems, protecting the integrity of information requires even more. Voters must have confidence that their vote is recorded accurately, and that the ballot is not altered after it is recorded. The best way to ensure votes are recorded accurately is through some kind of audit mechanism. Then, use of blockchain technology provides a nearly foolproof way of ensuring ballots are not altered once recorded. As a final step, election officials should empower designated third-party services to audit and certify the blockchain implementation.

In recent years, blockchain technology has surged onto the scene as a leading method for ensuring the integrity of transactional systems of all types, including electoral systems. West Virginia, Utah, and Colorado have all successfully implemented Voatz, a blockchain solution, for their absentee voting solution in recent elections. Understanding the mechanics of blockchain technology will clarify the potential of this new way to preserve voter confidence.

The "blocks" in a blockchain are basically payloads of encrypted information tagged with complex hash values. A hash value is a digital fingerprint for an electronic file--the unique result of running the file through a one-way algorithm. There are many different algorithms to produce hash values. Once a file has been hashed, any change to the file--no matter how small--will produce a radically different hash value. Therefore, when an encrypted file is sent with its hash value, the receiving station can confirm that the original file has not been changed by running the received file through the same hash function and comparing the hash value produced at the destination with the hash value that accompanied the file.

Inside each block are other hash values. There are individual hash values for some number of encrypted transactions, some metadata, a function called a "nonce" that is the trigger for closing out the block, and the completed hash for the entire contents of the preceding block. As each transaction is hashed and added to the block, all of the participating nodes in the blockchain system calculate the current hash of the entire contents of the block at that instant. When one of these calculated hash values reaches the trigger point designated by the nonce, the hash of that entire block is transmitted to the entire network. When the majority of participating nodes confirm that the block hash satisfies the requirement for completing the block, the block is added as the next block in the chain.

Even blockchain solutions must be audited. When the network of participating nodes is sufficiently centralized, as we might expect it to be in a state voting system, it is technically possible to insert one or more counterfeit blocks into the chain if a majority of the nodes concur. So, for instance, in my home state of Utah, with 29 counties and a finite, relatively small number of precincts, it is possible for some number of pre-built counterfeit blocks to be seeded by compromised nodes in a manner that would preempt legitimate blocks if a sufficient number of nodes were involved in the conspiracy. The only way to ensure that the election results are valid is an end-to-end audit that can tie specific election results to specific ballot transaction identifiers.

Given recent efforts by rogue state actors to create doubt about electoral processes using social media, the ability to perform an end-to-end audit of the voting process in a way that allows officials to certify election results in a credible manner is increasingly important to maintaining voter confidence. Systems to enable this type of audit by establishing a transaction id for each ballot were challenged several years ago on the basis that they violated voters' right to privacy. But a 2012 ruling in federal district court (*Citizens Center v. Gessler*) held that there is no constitutional right to a secret ballot. Given the need for an audit mechanism to protect the systems that guarantee our right to vote, it seems appropriate to me that the individual voter's right to privacy should be subordinate to legitimate mechanisms for providing a credible audit. It also seems to me that, beyond what is absolutely necessary to create a credible audit mechanism, the secrecy of the individual's voter data should be protected to the greatest extent possible.

In the context of election security, traditional information security combined with blockchain technology and appropriate auditing protocols can provide credible assurance that votes are accurately counted and protected from tampering. Given the demonstrated threat, it is important for all Americans to insist that the state officials responsible for the administration of elections take aggressive actions to implement comprehensive election security and auditing solutions.

CHAPTER 28

Increasing Voter Access

Originally published August 28, 2015.

What kinds of tools do we need to be amazing citizens? How can we make each registered voter believe their contribution is valued and important to the processes of our republic? Another part of my answer--the part I will discuss today--is access. We have to increase access to our political processes for our registered voters if we hope to inspire the levels of participation we need for a healthy republic.

You may be thinking, well, this is America, and we have all the access we need. The problem, you say, is that not enough people are taking advantage of the access we have. Okay, I agree that the problem is not enough people taking advantage of the access we have. By default, I submit that means we need more access for registered

Photo by Stephen Tryon

voters. We can judge people who don't vote today, but that is just a star-belly sneetch trap, and it doesn't solve the problem. Solving the problem requires some more understanding of what is causing the problem.

What factors discourage participation? Well, for one thing I think many people are just busy with higher priority tasks like family and work. The process of making an informed political choice is a time commitment, and many people simply do not make that commitment. To the extent we could reduce the time required to make an informed choice, or give people more time to make that choice, we would encourage participation. This is the low-hanging fruit of improving our republic, and it is why I advocate improving the technology and content of congressional web sites.

Another discouraging factor is that an overwhelming number of congressional districts today are solidly one-party districts. In other words, the districts have been re-drawn by one party or the other so that there is little chance of the minority party winning an election. The most recent estimate I have seen in the *New York Times* is that 400 of the 435 congressional districts are now solidly one-party districts (Edsall). Faced with what is essentially an inevitable outcome, some minority party voters in these districts simply consider it a waste of time to vote. If you are a Republican in a gerrymandered Democratic district, or a Democrat in a gerrymandered Republican district, you are effectively disenfranchised. Restoring districts where each party has a real chance at winning an election would encourage participation.

What makes one-party districts even more toxic for our republic is the fact that the candidates appearing on the final ballot are determined in primaries that exclude independent voters. In other words, the 40+ percent of registered voters who refuse to align with either the Democratic or Republican party are not allowed to participate in the primary elections paid for with their tax dollars. Those voters are then confronted with a general election where the majority candidate--a candidate they could not help select--is assured victory. The 40+ percent of registered voters who refuse to align with either the Democratic or Republican party are effectively disenfranchised.

Access enables participation. Although it is certainly our individual responsibility to vote and to participate appropriately in the political processes of our republic, our elected officials can do a number of things to encourage--or discourage--participation. Participation goes up the more we make our political processes accessible: accessible to busy Americans who correctly prioritize taking care of their families and jobs over babysitting the people they elect and pay to caretake our government.

Many politicians are more interested in preserving the status quo than increasing the accessibility of our political processes. Elected officials should take it as part of their jobs, in my opinion, to encourage good citizenship and promote accessibility so more Americans exercise their right to vote. The reason I emphasize electing career citizens over career politicians is that career citizens won't be afraid to make increasing access a priority. We should measure elected officials by their willingness to increase access for registered voters and by the percentage of registered voters in their districts who actually vote.

Not all elected officials see it as part of their job to encourage political participation. A few years ago, I had lunch with my representative, Jason Chaffetz. I pitched the idea of real-time polling on his web site as a way of increasing voter participation. In support of the idea, I lamented the fact that, because they were so busy with work and family, many people just didn't make time for politics and wound up acting like sheep. His response: "If people want to be sheep, we should let them be sheep." My concern is that many people unintentionally let themselves become sheep because they are busy. We can and should do things to make participation more accessible for these people. For Jason, increasing political participation is simply not a priority.

About 38 percent of the registered voters in Jason's district voted in the last election. Even though an overwhelming majority--72 percent--of that 38 percent voted for Jason, it is hard for me to accept that we let 27 percent of the registered voters in my district (72 percent of 38 percent) choose our congressman. We let 27 percent of registered voters--that's less than one-third--choose our congressman because 62 percent of registered voters didn't exercise their right to vote. I was one of the unaffiliated candidates (running without a party affiliation) running against Jason in that election, and he got a whole lot more votes than I did. That probably would have been the case even if more people had voted. Statisticians would tell you it certainly would have been the case. But the fact is we just don't know, because 62 percent of the people who could have voted did not.

I listened to a conference call recently about the Open Our Democracy Act. This bill has been re-introduced in the current Congress. The bill would go a long way toward increasing voter participation by addressing the three causes of non-participation discussed above. For one thing, the bill would make election day a national holiday. Imagine the power of that simple change! People would have a chance to finish their research and go to the polls without missing work. Frankly, I can think of few things more worth celebrating with a day off work than our ability to vote.

The Open Our Democracy Act would also require Top Two non-partisan primaries. Top-Two primaries are primary elections in which everyone can vote, even if they are not registered with the Democratic or Republican parties. The two candidates receiving the highest number of votes would then be the only candidates appearing on the general election ballot, again without regard to their political affiliation.

Finally, the Open Our Democracy Act would have the General Accounting Office study the idea of national standards for drawing the lines around congressional districts in order to make them less susceptible to manipulation by political parties. In my opinion, it would be best if each state fixed the problem of gerrymandering on their own, but a GAO study would help arm citizens in each state with the information they need to start state reform movements. The results of a GAO study are not law—it is just information to support the process of law-making. Gerrymandering has been part of our political landscape from the earliest days of our country, but that does not mean we should continue to tolerate this increasingly toxic activity. Many reasons suggest that the effects of gerrymandering--effectively disenfranchising large numbers of registered voters--is more harmful today than at any time in our history. It is time to begin the process of addressing gerrymandered districts.

All three elements of the Open Our Democracy Act would, in my view, increase accessibility and participation in the democratic processes of our republic. We cannot carry out our individual duty to vote if we do not have appropriate access to the political processes that make our individual vote meaningful. We have allowed our access to be degraded to the point where access to the democratic processes of our republic is largely an illusion for most registered voters. Our elected officials should be doing everything in their power to increase accessibility and participation. The best litmus test to distinguish career citizens from career politicians is full and unconditional support for the Open Our Democracy Act. Career citizens will support it. Career politicians will try to stop it.

CHAPTER 29

The Best Way to Redistrict

Originally published February 19, 2021.

It should be a given: we should all agree every American citizen should be equal in the eyes of our law and our government. That is the promise of the equal protection clause in the Fourteenth Amendment of our Constitution. If we truly believe all should be equal before the law, then we must also support systems that expand informed participation by our fellow citizens in our political process to the greatest extent possible. Legislative districts that are drawn improperly effectively disenfranchise large numbers of our fellow citizens across the political spectrum. Such districts are widespread and, I believe, unconstitutional.

Given that seats in the United States House of Representatives are apportioned based on population at the state level, it seems self evident to me that any given state's delegation should reflect the party alignment of that state's voters. When this is not the case because of districts that have been drawn to favor a particular party, we can describe the districts as gerrymandered. The Washington Post presented a succinct explanation of the issue several years ago ("Gerrymandering"). District alignment with registered voter party affiliation in a state is, or should be, a given. I will not argue further for that first principle in this essay. Rather, I will use this essay to argue for a second, subordinate principle: we should draw all legislative districts to maximize informed participation in our political process.

It seems obvious that the overwhelming number of one-party districts is a major cause of the gridlock we are experiencing with our federal government. A few years ago, the New York Times reported that over 400 of the 435 congressional districts were dominated by a large majority of one party (Edsall). In these districts, the nominee of the majority party is virtually guaranteed to win the general election. Minority party voters are essentially disenfranchised. One-party districts reward candidates for appealing to the extreme members of their party who are reliable voters in primary elections. Ultimately, even moderate members of the majority party can be disenfranchised. Members of Congress from one-party districts have no incentive to compromise with the other party in the halls of Congress.

Figure 1: This map shows the Utah Congressional Districts after the 2000 census.

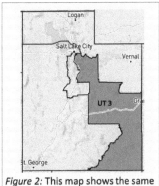

Figure 2: This map shows the same districts after the 2010 census.

Screenshot from Utah.gov website

It's bad enough that one-party districts produce Members of Congress unwilling to compromise, but they also enable public officials who do not have to care about what most of their constituents think. I live in a one-party district. In 2014, I suggested to my representative that he should modify his web site to better engage and inform people. My fear,

I said, was that people did not have time to chase down the information necessary to be informed citizens, so they just wound up being sheep. His response: "We should let them be sheep." There is no motivation for majority-party incumbents in one-party districts to improve the level of civic engagement and participation in their districts. Worse yet, there is little motivation for minority party voters in such districts to participate.

If we believe in our Constitution, and in the six purposes for our federal government enumerated therein, then building better legislative districts is one of the most important structural reforms we can accomplish. We can rebuild legislative districts at all levels to support the broadest possible scope of informed participation by our fellow citizens. After ensuring that state delegations reflect the party affiliations of registered voters in a state, we should strive to create districts where every voter feels their vote can make a difference. Balanced districts, or districts with the closest possible balance between the parties, will provide incentives for all parties to encourage informed participation by the greatest number of our fellow citizens.

CHAPTER 30

A Litmus Test for Elected Public Servants

Originally published July 31, 2015.

I am swimming against the current a little bit here. Most of the news these days is focused on next year's presidential election. It is certainly important that we choose our next Chief Executive wisely, and with a large number of candidates running in both major parties, choosing one at this point can be a bit daunting. What I am saying about the qualities we should look for in our elected officials in general does have some bearing on the presidential election.

In fact, this investigation of criteria for re-election led directly to the article "What Makes a Great President" in my summer (2015) newsletter. That article discusses a criterion that correlates with presidential greatness, a criterion that correlates with below-average performance in the White House, and a criterion that--perhaps surprisingly for some--doesn't seem to matter. But in this post I want to ex-

AccountabilityCitizenship.org's "stoplight" logo
Photo by Stephen Tryon

amine a more general case. I want to consider what may be the right criteria for deciding whether to vote for any official. I am proposing a model where the traits that favor a candidate are the traits of what I call a career citizen. On the other hand, career politician is my label for the collection of traits that indicates someone is unfit for public office. What differentiates a career citizen from a career politician?

First of all, elected officials should be public servants. We have collective amnesia on what a public servant is, and we tolerate too many people in elected office who are self servants on the public payroll. A public servant serves the people they represent--all of them--regardless of their political party or whether they made a campaign donation. Some of you are thinking, well, if an elected official doesn't put donors or members of their own party first, they won't get re-elected. But as soon as we allow elected officials to put their own re-election ahead of their duty to the public that they serve, we have decided to lower the standard for public service. We have decided to accept public officials who do their duty only when it doesn't hurt their chances for re-election. When we accept politicians putting their own tenure or benefit ahead of their duty to the public good, the public good will always be a secondary concern.

Second, elected officials should be completely beyond reproach in their performance of duty. That doesn't mean that everyone has to like everything an elected official does: popularity is not the same thing as being beyond reproach in the performance of one's duty. Performing one's duty in a manner that is beyond reproach means being 100 percent transparent (honest and clear) about what you are doing and why. It means being able to articulate how your actions are related to the duties you have been elected to carry out.

Again, we have allowed ourselves to grow complacent and accept a low standard of honor and duty in many of our public officials. In Utah, for instance, two recent state attorneys general were brought up on felony charges for accepting bribes and selling influence. Although both were acquitted, the behavior that led to the charges made their acquittal seem like a technicality. My point here is that true public servants have no business engaging in any behavior that is even close to bribery or influence peddling. When it comes to the laws that cover bribery and selling influence, we should not tolerate behavior that is anywhere close to being illegal in a public official. If your behavior is close enough to the line between legality and illegality that you can be indicted for five or ten felonies, you have NO business being a public official.

Accepting gifts while in public office is an absolute non-starter. That is why federal officials are restricted from giving or receiving gifts above a token value and must turn over to the federal government anything received above that value. As a young Army officer, I was taught the "headline test." If you are about to do something that you would be un-comfortable reading as a headline in the New York Times or the Washington Post, then you have no business doing it as long as you are a public official.

This last point bears repeating. We should not tolerate public offi-cials who behave in a way that is just barely legal. We want public of-ficials who are scrupulously honest, even to the point of hurting their chances for re-election. Last month, a story about the scandal involving the two former Utah attorneys general carried the headline "Make Mike Lee our guy". Mike Lee (R) is a United States Senator from Utah. One of the people involved in the corruption trial against one of the former attorney generals claimed that attorney general was bundling campaign contributions--giving money to people so they could donate it to Mike Lee in order to circumvent the federal law restricting individual contri-butions ("Feds... allege Johnson illegally donated to Mike Lee...").

The article was quick to point out that Mike Lee didn't know about the illegal bundling, and that is great. The question that arose in my mind, though, was how the illegal contributions could "make Mike Lee our guy" unless at some point, someone intended to let him know they represented some dollar amount of contributions. I understand that conversation would not implicate Mike Lee in any wrongdoing as long as Lee understood the individual contributions were legitimate and not the product of illegal bundling.

My point here is that, regardless of the legalities involved, career cit-izens would respond very differently than career politicians to someone claiming to represent some dollar amount of contributions. A career citizen would respond by saying something like, "Thanks for your contribution. You know I don't condone or practice pay-as-you-go politics, but I hope you are happy enough with my performance in support of all the citizens in our city/county/state to support me in the next election as well."

A career politician, on the other hand, might behave so as to indicate that donors got special treatment as a result of their donation(s). Maybe donors letters get answered when others do not. Maybe legislative priorities mirror the priorities of certain donors. Those are behaviors that wink at corruption, even though they may be technically legal in and of themselves. In sum, a career citizen demonstrates a pattern of selflessness--putting the welfare of others before their own welfare--while a career politician demonstrates a pattern of taking care of themselves, especially their re-election, as a top priority.

Why am I spending so much time talking about corruption? After all, this is America, right? Sure, we have our scandals, but we don't really have a corruption problem, do we? Yes we do, at least in my humble opinion. Let's look at the most obvious examples in recent years: Rod Blagojevich (D), 40th Governor of Illinois, began serving a 14-year prison term in 2012 for corruption. Blagojevich was elected 3 times to the United States House of Representatives before spending 6 years as the governor of Illinois before being impeached. Donald Trump (R) pardoned Blagojevich (D) in 2020 while downplaying his blatant corruption ("Trump commutes sentence...").

You may remember Dan Rostenkowski (D). He was the representative in the same district for 36 years and was chairman of one of the most powerful committees in the U.S. Congress before pleading guilty and serving time in prison for mail fraud in 1996 ("Rostenkowski sentenced..."). How about Bob McDonnell (R), remember him? He was the governor of Virginia from 2010 to 2014. He was indicted on federal charges ten days after leaving office and convicted a few months later of accepting improper gifts and loans while in office ("...Mcdonnell found guilty..."). Before becoming governor, by the way, McDonnell served as the attorney general for Virginia, and before that he was a member of Virginia's House of Delegates for 14 years. And let's not forget Denny Hastert (R), the longest serving Republican Speaker of the U.S. House of Representatives, who became the highest-ranking elected official in U.S. history to have served a prison sentence when he was convicted in 2015. Hastert was convicted of financial crimes committed after he left office. He committed those crimes while trying to cover up child molestation crimes committed before he was elected to Congress ("Dennis Hastert sentenced...").

These are not peripheral, no-name, skulk-in-the-shadows perpetrators. They are main-line politicians of both major political parties serving as elected officials in important state and federal government positions for long periods of time. If you think they just all-of-a-sudden crossed a line or lost sight of the law, I think you are naive. It is far more likely these people engaged in a long-term pattern of increasingly corrupt behavior that eventually became so obvious that they found themselves facing charges. We have a corruption problem in public politics, America, and we need to make it our top priority to elect career citizens who demonstrate the willingness not just to live within the law, but the passion for setting an example of selfless and honorable public service.

How do we know who to vote for? Well, first of all, I would say do not vote for people who have demonstrated long-term success in politics. Not all such people are bad, of course, but we have to understand that politics, like war, is a morally toxic endeavor. We should, therefore, elect people who have become successful outside of politics, and we should insist that our elected public servants remove themselves from public office and return to private employment or business for reasonable stretches of time.

This is not a matter of kicking people out of office because they have done poorly. It is a matter of forcing people to take a break from the morally toxic environment of politics. Perhaps they can return at a later time, and perhaps not. That is not the point. Remember, we are talking about elected public servants, not people who are elected to look after their own careers in politics.

Term limits? Sure. But how about we just all decide we aren't going to re-elect the same people over and over? The Constitution gives us the power to change 87 percent of Congress every two years, but we re-elect incumbents in about 90 percent of the races where they choose to seek re-election. You want better, more honest government? Elect people who have earned--not inherited--their own success in the private sector, and don't let them stay in office for more than a few years at a time.

Well, you say, I am a Democrat or a Republican, and the only way I can vote for candidates who believe what I believe is to vote for the candidate who shares my party affiliation, and the only candidates in my party are those who are long-term incumbents. So really, I don't have a choice--I have to vote for the incumbent, right?

No, you don't. You have to accept that it is more important to elect someone fresh than it is to elect someone who claims to think like you do. After all, it is not the case that any elected official waltzes into office and immediately succeeds in getting all of their political beliefs enshrined into law. We have ponderous bureaucracies that ensure our government does not reflect the views of any one public official. Electing someone who is fresh is more important to restoring honest, open and efficient government than electing someone who claims to think like you. Oh, and by the way, people who get elected because they claim to think the way the majority of their constituents think might not be the best people to elect in the first place. Think about it.

I believe the question we should ask everyone seeking public office is this: "what is the most important view you hold that runs against the popular opinion of your party, and what are your reasons for holding that view?" This is a litmus test because it forces someone to either take a real risk or to play it safe. People who play it safe and claim to support their party in every respect are not fit to be public servants.

That is why the picture at the top of this page shows a green "go" light around citizenship and a red "stop" light around partisanship. People who cannot speak intelligently about an important issue where their personal views diverge from the prevailing opinion of their political "team" lack either moral courage or intellect. It is just that simple. No one should agree with everything a political party stands for in every instance.

So that's it! Running for office against an entrenched incumbent is a sacrifice. We need career citizens--credible people with real track records of merit-based success outside of politics--to volunteer to run for office now more than ever. When it comes time to decide between candidates, we need to favor challengers over incumbents. We need to look closely for behavior-based evidence of character and selflessness.

Character and selflessness in this context are measured by the demonstrated willingness to make the good of a business or other non-political organization a higher priority than one's personal interests. Claims of religiosity or political affiliation are not evidence of character. Such claims are cheap and often counterfeit. For me, the candidate who gets my vote is the non-incumbent with a record of serving others who offers the best answer to the question: "what is the most important view you hold that runs against the popular opinion of your party, and what are your reasons for holding that view?"

Study Questions and Key Terms

1. Has technology changed the knowledge, skills and attributes needed for effective citizenship in the American republic? Why or why not?
2. Has technology changed the authority needed by the government to fulfill the purposes enumerated in the Constitution? Why or why not?
3. Using deductive form, write out an argument that captures the case made in Essay 28 in support of using systems to expand informed access and participation in political processes by all citizens.
4. In Essay 30, there is an inductive argument supporting the conclusion that America has a corruption problem in public politics. Write out the premises and conclusion of this inductive argument. Can you also put the argument in deductive form? How?
5. How are congressional districts determined? What is meant by the statement, "We should not allow politicians to pick their voters"? Do you agree or disagree with this statement?

KEY TERMS

1. **six purposes of government** -- In the United States Constitution, the six purposes given for our government are to "form a more perfect Union, establish Justice, insure domestic Tranquility, provide for the common defence, promote the general Welfare, and secure the Blessings of Liberty to ourselves and our Posterity."
2. **effective population density** – A measurement intended to represent the need for government services at a point in time. The mea-

surement is determined by taking the total population, dividing it by total area in square miles, then multiplying the result (quotient) by the average speed of information in miles per hour and multiplying again by a technology factor representing ability of population to physically access information.

3. **government regulation** - A rule, directive or law made and enforced by a governmental entity.

4. **scope of governmental authority** – The extent to which government regulation is appropriate with regard to subject matter, intrusion into individual privacy, and constraints.

5. **public servant** - A person elected, appointed or hired into a position with a duty to provide a service to the public.

6. **Voter Transparency Tool** – Information system to augment congressional websites, increasing access by registered voters to information about the quality of their public servants.

7. **multifactor authentication** - The use of more than one piece of information over more than one device or channel in order to permit access to a resource or space.

8. **voter registration** – The process that validates a person's eligibility to vote.

9. **confidentiality, integrity and availability** – Three goals of information system security that refer to keeping information safe from unauthorized access, unauthorized changes, and unauthorized interference with access by approved users at approved times.

10. **information system security** – Principles, procedures and technologies, often used in a layered approach, to protect the confidentiality, integrity and availability of information systems.

11. **blockchain** - A technology to protect the integrity of information by combining elements of timestamped, fingerprinted information into clusters that are also timestamped and fingerprinted.

12. **hash** – A one-way algorithm for generating a unique digital fingerprint for electronic files.

13. **gerrymandering** - changing the boundaries of a district to provide political advantage to one group.

14. **Open Our Democracy Act** – bill introduced in Congress in 2017 that would make election day a federal holiday, require open and top-two primary elections, and end gerrymandering by regulation of redistricting.
15. **redistricting**- a process for redrawing districts based on results from the census.

VI

PART VI

Conclusions

Bottom Line Up Front

We humans seem unable to resolve our chronic cycles of conflict. The firmware of our brains speeds our response to potential threats but also biases our interpretation of the world around us. We tend to value personal concerns more heavily than concerns that affect others. Yet we are social animals. We need others to compensate for our bias and maximize our freedom as well as for biological reasons. Throughout history, great thinkers have diagnosed this tension between self-interest and our social nature. Still, we confront the same challenge today that we find in Socrates' dialogue with Callicles: how do you sustain a healthy society when some people define virtue as self-interest? Essay 31 asserts that virtues of humility and tolerance, along with systems to encourage compromise are key to balancing self-interest with the dignity and rights of all citizens.

CHAPTER 31

People Who Disagree With You About Politics Aren't Necessarily Evil

Empanadas could be a metaphor for all we share as humans.
Photo by Stephen Tryon

Originally published 6/10/2018 as *Life is Like an Empanada...*

I was at a party recently for a friend who was using his birthday as a fundraiser for refugees resetting in our state. A number of refugee-run food preparation businesses, some still in the incubator stage, provided an amazing array of tasty treats for the soiree. I had just finished my second run at some of the delicious fare when I spotted another friend across the room, and made my way over to say hi. After exchanging pleasantries and agreeing the food was magnificent, my friend observed, "Isn't it amazing that every culture in the world has figured out that, if you take some meat and seasoning, wrap it in dough of some sort, and fry it, it tastes great?"

Well, it is kind of amazing. We have a lot in common as human beings. Each of us carries about three billion of the genetic building blocks that make us who we are. Of that astronomical amount of biological information, only about one-tenth of one percent is unique to us as individuals. The rest—99.9 percent—is the same for all of us. Black, white, straight, gay, Republican, Democrat, Arab, Jew, Hindu, Buddhist or Christian: all are 99.9 percent the same from a genetic standpoint ("Our dna...").

Given this overwhelming similarity, it has always struck me as odd that we persecute each other so much over our differences. Over time, the more I thought about it, the odder it seemed. Then it dawned on me. Philosophers and scientists have recognized, deliberated and opined for thousands of years on this exact subject. Many great thinkers agree that, among the many characteristics we share with other human beings, we share characteristics that encourage our propensity for disagreement and conflict. We share physical and psychological mechanisms for seeing the world imperfectly (from our individual perspective), for overvaluing our imperfect individual perspectives and opinions, and for responding with hostility to those who look, think and act differently than ourselves. That hostile response is ingrained; it is born of reflexive heuristics that have been critical to our survival as a species over tens of thousands of years.

But the shared evolutionary mechanisms and cognitive heuristics that have enabled our survival to this point are now a threat to our survival. From climate change to terrorism to the threat of a nuclear, biological, chemical or environmental catastrophe, the challenges to which we must respond demand cooperation on a global scale. We cannot hope to be successful with international cooperation unless we can first solve

Photo by Stephen Tryon

the challenge of cooperation in the political arena within the United States of America.

Our Constitution provides us the institutional mechanisms necessary to achieve the required level of cooperation. But institutional mechanisms reflect the values of the people we elect to make them work. Too many of us are failing to practice the social virtues our founders warned us would be necessary for our republic to survive (Fitzpatrick, 29:410). We are electing too many people who manifest this same lack of social virtue in the way they represent their constituents. If we are to achieve the level of cooperation necessary for our survival, we must transcend our evolutionary legacy. We must acknowledge the tendency for bias we all inherit as human beings, and we must strive to elect officials who will serve the public good with humility, tolerance and a spirit of compromise (Sparks, 10: 297).

A Cognitive Legacy Defined Through the Ages

In the western tradition, some of the earliest philosophers to figure out the social challenge presented by our imperfect individual perceptions of the world were Socrates, Plato and Aristotle. As it happened, Plato was a student of Socrates, and Aristotle was a student of Plato. Ironically, in spite of similarities in their views on the social aspect of human nature, these great thinkers took the human tendency to err and went in different directions with it.

Socrates lived in the fifth century BC and was a citizen of Athens. He fought for Athens with distinction in several battles. Apart from his military service, he never left Athens. He is known as a philosopher and teacher through the writings of others, especially Plato. Socrates believed human action was motivated by happiness, and that virtue and knowledge were important to achieving happiness. Socrates linked happiness and virtue to our social natures and our duties as citizens. He would often start from a position of humility, asserting that the only thing he knew was that he knew nothing. He would then proceed to use definitions and questions about fundamental values to illuminate conceptual and ethical weaknesses in common beliefs and practices (Guthrie 80).

Eventually, Socrates' questions created enough anger among those he was obliquely criticizing to get him in trouble. By this time, the Athenian democracy had decayed into an oligarchy of tyrants. Socrates was arrested, tried and sentenced to die. In Plato's dialogue *Crito*, which describes Socrates' conversations with his friends on the day before his execution, Socrates refuses Crito's offer to pay for his escape and life in exile. He argues such an escape would undermine the laws of Athens, to which he owes all the benefits he has enjoyed in life (49-54). Combined with the example given in the dialogue *Apology*, wherein Socrates refuses to follow an order from the tyrants to unjustly seize a fellow citizen for execution, Socrates' submission to his own death sentence is a powerful testimony to our duties as social animals, both to our government and to our fellow citizens (32: c-e).

Plato also asserted a strong connection between our individual virtue and our role in society. In Book II of *Republic*, he says we could better see and understand individual virtue by viewing it first as it would appear in an ideal state (368-69). Later, in Book VII, Plato uses the allegory of the cave to support the notion that the only unchanging reality is in the realm of ideas. In a very general sense, we can say that Plato placed the locus of error and disagreement in an over reliance on our senses, which can only provide us a distorted, shadowy projection of the ideal. Plato held that our only path to truly see and understand the Ideal Forms in the realm of ideas was through perfecting our rational capacity. Not everyone was capable of honing their reason sufficiently to see the Forms, so it was important for society to carefully select and train those who had this capacity. These people could then guide the rest of the population to the best possible understanding of the Forms (514-520). Achieving the highest possible understanding of the Forms was essential for society because Plato thought the ideal Forms had power—to the extent that people had knowledge of the Form of Good, for instance, they would be motivated to act in accordance with it. For Plato, the source of disagreement and conflict was our imperfect development of our rational capacity and the resulting distortions in our perception of the good.

Aristotle's empiricism, on the other hand, embraces the imperfection of sense as a part of our human way of being. The only reality, for Aristotle, was the reality presented to us by our senses, as imperfect as those senses might be. His tireless study of the world around him led him to posit the notion that living things were combinations of form and substance--each living thing possessed a form or blueprint of sorts that caused its physical matter to change in accordance with its purpose or function. Human beings' purpose and function were tied to our nature as social animals with senses and a capacity for reason. The proper use of reason was to balance emotions, desires and the imperfections of our senses to achieve virtue, which for Aristotle was often a mean between the possible extremes of human behavior. Realizing individual virtue would also make a person an exemplary citizen in a virtuous society. For Aristotle, the source of conflict and disagreement was a failure to achieve proper human virtue (Aristotle xiii-xxiv).

Two thousand years later, Immanuel Kant presented a synthesis of sorts. Kant introduces the notion that the limits to our experience are in place before experience--a priori--and are insurmountable. Kant was an idealist--he agreed with Plato that our senses were a filter that prevented direct experience of the phenomena that cause our sensory experience. However, he denied that reason could gain access to phenomena (Kant 82). Instead, in a nod to Aristotle, Kant used reason to construct an argument for a master ethical rule that applied to the world of perception--the world as we experience it. He called his rule the Categorical Imperative. Basically, Kant's idea was that people should act in a way that they could universalize. But the important point for me in Kant's thinking is the notion that the limits to our ability to reason are pre-cognitive.

The fact that Kant introduced these limits as pre-cognitive "forms of intuition" was a big deal for him--he referred to it as a "Copernican revolution" in ethical thinking. The implications are interesting: at least some of the limits to our perceptions are not a function of individual virtue, intellect or choice. But we are still left with the challenge of reasoning to a shared conception of the Good based on different individual circumstances and perspectives within the common constraints of human experience. There is ample room for different interpretations of the Form of the Good, or the virtues of a good citizen, or even the Categorical Imperative.

A Modern Twist

When you combine the notion of precognitive constraints with modern psychology and economics, things get more interesting. Thomas Sowell's notion of conflicting visions and Daniel Kahneman's arguments for the role of evolutionary forces in shaping various precognitive response mechanisms open the door to the notion that, not only are we built to get things wrong as individuals, but even the differences in how we tend to get things wrong are a function of systems that operate more as a reflex than as a function of intentional reason.

Economist Thomas Sowell used a conflict between two archetypal "visions"--a constrained vision and an unconstrained vision--to explain the way people judge issues and events. He further defined the concept of a vision as a "pre-analytic cognitive act," and, later, as "a set of assumptions not necessarily spelled out even in the individual's own mind" (Sowell 96-108). Sowell's visions can be seen as a metaphor of sorts for an individual's instinctive decision paradigms.

Daniel Kahneman, a research psychologist who won the 2002 Nobel Prize in economics for his work on decision-making, uses several metaphors of his own to present a fascinating look at our decision-making processes. In his book, *Thinking, Fast and Slow*, Kahneman describes "systematic errors in the thinking of normal people" which his research shows are the result of "the design of the machinery of cognition rather than... the corruption of thought by emotion." He uses "System 1" to describe our fast response mechanism that relies more heavily on emotion and heuristics (models) to simplify our complex world and enable us to react in the way most likely to keep us safe. System 2, on the other hand, is slower and engages the ability to reason to a much greater extent, while still accepting inputs from emotions and cognitive models (35).

The cognitive systems Kahneman describes are broadly shared, but at least some of the content of cognitive models, like availability and anchoring, vary based on individual and group experiences. It is like the child's toy that pushes blocks of clay through forms to create exotic shapes: the forms are the same but the color varies based on the type of clay that is put into the toy. One's level of education affords no necessary immunity to the error-inducing effects of our cognitive machinery. However, an understanding of the nature of the biases built into our systems of thought, along with conscious attention to mitigating those biases, can help.

The implications of all this are powerful. Rather than getting angry at those with different political views, we should acknowledge that those views are produced by cognitive machinery we share, coupled with System 1 inputs that may well be more reflexive than intentional. Our own views are as likely to be based on erroneous inputs as those with whom we disagree. The best path to reduce our collective errors is to ensure all views are considered in the light of a common understanding of our biases. The master virtues of our republic should be humility and tolerance, and our political processes should aim for compromise rather than dominance.

Study Questions and Key Terms

1. What is the author's argument explaining our human tendency for conflict given our overwhelmingly similar biological makeup?
2. Is biological similarity necessary or sufficient for peaceful coexistence? Why or why not?
3. How have cognitive mechanisms like availability and anchoring contributed to the survival of the human species.
4. How do the imperfections inherent in our individual perceptions support an argument for social virtues of humility and tolerance?

KEY TERMS

1. **evolution** – Evolution is a process of change in biological characteristics of species over time due to natural selection.
2. **genetic makeup** – An individual's genetic makeup, or genotype, refers to the sequence of DNA in their cells that is analogous to the blueprint for that individual's body.
3. **self-interest** – A term that refers to one's personal advantage or well-being, and that is often used in the context of behavior that lacks appropriate consideration for the interests of others.
4. **social good** – A social good is something recognized as advantageous to the majority of the population or, in some cases, to all of the population. Clean water is an example of a social good.
5. **Categorical Imperative** – The Categorical Imperative is the central precept of Immanual Kant's 19th century moral philosophy, which

holds that people should only act on principles that they could will to be universal laws.

6. **vision** – According to economist Thomas Sowell, a vision is a pre-cognitive framework of assumptions about how the world works. Sowell argues that visions are often taken as a given, and that conflicts between visions can explain persistent patterns of disagreement in society.

7. **pre-cognitive** – This term refers to something that is given to us before thought experience or sensory input. This can include fore-knowledge of events or subjects before any experience of those events or subjects.

8. **decision paradigm** – Decision paradigms are processes or frameworks used to make choices between competing alternatives.

9. **anchoring** – Also called the anchoring effect, anchoring is a form of cognitive bias that influences a person's decisions based on some particular reference point, especially when the person's decision would have been different in the absence of that reference point.

10. **firmware** – In computers, firmware is permanent software programmed into a read-only memory. By analogy, one could refer to our pre-cognitive decision paradigms as the firmware of our human brains.

APPENDIX 1: A PRIMER ON CRITICAL REASONING

This book is a praxis—a practical exercise in critical reasoning. It assumes, therefore, that the reader has some innate or acquired ability to distinguish what is reasonable from what is not reasonable. This appendix presents basic principles that should guide the process of critical reasoning. It is a resource for those who have never considered how they arrive at conclusions they find reasonable. It can also serve as a refresher for those who have not considered such a methodology recently, and a Rosetta Stone, of sorts, for those seeking to understand how the process of critical reasoning used in this book maps to their own.

By way of definition, critical reasoning is the process of marshaling evidence to justify conclusions. The evidence is usually in the form of premises or descriptions of the world we experience. A set of premises and its conclusion may be called an argument. Throughout the book, requirements to identify arguments presented in the readings are simply requirements to explicitly identify a set of premises that support a specific conclusion (or are believed to support that conclusion).

Identifying premises and conclusions is an important skill. You and I are unlikely to reach agreement if you think I am using premises x and y to support conclusion z while I think I am using premises a and b to support conclusion c. The requirement to diagram arguments is, therefore, a recurring task in this book. In Appendix 2, the author presents diagrams of some specific arguments identified in the Study Questions at the end of each section.

The fact that the argument you diagram in a specific case is not exactly the same as the argument shown in Appendix 2 does not necessarily mean your argument is incorrect. There are different ways to diagram any given argument. Indeed, it is possible to find different arguments in any piece of moderately complex reasoning. The author recommends that solutions be judged on the basis of whether the text provides reasonable support for the argument as diagrammed.

An Argument is a Set of Premises That Support a Conclusion

Premise 1: All fish are animals with gills.
Premise 2: All trout are fish.
Conclusion: All trout are animals with gills.

Figure 1

There is that word "reasonable." Whatever does it mean? For our purposes, let us agree that "reasonable" refers to a world of shared experience. Within this world, your perceptions of our shared experience may differ from my perceptions in some cases, but should agree with my perceptions in other cases. We call things more or less reasonable as a matter of shared judgment based on available evidence. What is reasonable or unreasonable depends on whether the nature of our shared experience is more factual or subjective as well as on the quality and quantity of factual evidence that supports one view or the other.

Imagine we walk into a room together. Consider the spectrum of experiences we share in the room. We should be able to agree on something like whether the light is on or off. That is a matter of fact.

If you tell me that the room is cold, however, we may disagree. If we have a thermometer, we can agree on the temperature that it shows, but I cannot judge whether your subjective experience of "cold" is reasonable or unreasonable without further information. And even if I establish that the room itself is not cold, I must still allow that your subjective experience of feeling cold is accurate (and perhaps caused by something other than the ambient temperature).

Now imagine that the wall of our room features a framed picture of a fully clothed woman in a tight-fitting blouse and holding a pitcher of beer. Or, if you prefer, the picture depicts a well-muscled and shirtless man holding the same pitcher. You may label the picture as pornographic. I might protest and say it is just an advertisement for a popular brand of beer. On further discussion, we might agree that it is "reasonable" to display the picture next to the menu on the wall of a tavern, but not on the wall of a house of worship. Our different views in this case are more a matter of personal values than a matter of fact or perception.

Increasingly, our public discourse is polarized and marked by an inability to agree on what is reasonable. One cause of this polarization could be that people are placing too much weight on their subjective perceptions and values rather than on matters of fact. Critical reasoning is a way to reclaim the area where compromise is possible by following a shared process that balances facts with the validity of subjective perceptions and values.

I should note here that reasonable arguments use premises that accurately model the world we live in. If you insist on using a premise about pigs that can fly under their own power, I will dismiss that premise and any conclusion based on it as unreasonable. There are no such pigs. I've not seen them, and I am confident you haven't either. In fact, if you insist on a premise that pigs can fly under their own power, it is more reasonable for me to assume you are deluded or deceived than to accept your premise. Such a premise does not accurately model the world we live in, and therefore has no place in the process of critical reasoning.

A Shared Process

Evaluating an argument is the process of identifying whether the evidence presented provides reasonable support for the conclusion. It is important to understand that an argument can be reasonable even if you do not agree with the conclusion. In any case, you should consider the strongest possible argument supported by the evidence in order to have the best chance of achieving either consensus on a conclusion or a compromise.

A good method for evaluating an argument is to start by identifying what the person presenting the case wants you to believe as a result of her efforts. In other words, what conclusion does the author attempt to support? What statements does the author use to support this conclusion? In the best case, the person presenting the argument gives a clear thesis statement. A thesis statement states the conclusion the author wants to support.

Anyone who has taught frosh composition at the college level can tell you that the conclusion the author wants to support is not always the conclusion best supported by the evidence they present. Authors sometimes don't know what conclusion they want to support, or spend so much effort addressing peripheral issues that they never clearly make the case for the conclusion they have in mind. It is useful, therefore, to start off by identifying one or more conclusions that the author seems to be trying to establish.

Inductive Reasoning and Deductive Reasoning

Once you have identified the conclusion or conclusions that the person presenting the argument is trying to support, it is useful to determine whether the author is using inductive reasoning or deductive reasoning. Both forms of reasoning can provide a strong foundation for an argument. A skilled practitioner of critical reasoning can formulate arguments using either inductive or deductive reasoning, and will choose the method that provides the best support for the conclusion.

Inductive reasoning moves from an examination of specific cases to conclusions that are likely with regard to the class or classes from which the specific cases are taken. This form of reasoning is the basis for the scientific method: we observe the world, form a hypothesis to explain our observations, and seek confirmation of our hypothesis with further observation. Confirming observations can increase the level of confidence we have in our hypothesis up to the point of near certainty. It is always possible that some new observation will force us to modify or replace our hypothesis. For this reason, we say that conclusions supported by inductive reasoning are always susceptible to epistemic uncertainty—the possibility that we simply do not yet know something that might better support a different conclusion.

For example, for over a hundred years, scientists believed they could explain all observable behavior of matter with four fundamental forces. These four forces were thought to be electromagnetic force, gravitational force, strong nuclear force and weak nuclear force. In recent years, experiments and observations have led many to assert that the evidence supports a model with five fundamental forces rather than four. The nature of the fifth force is still a matter of conjecture. However, if observations and particle behavior that would support a five-force model can be confirmed, then it is likely that the five-force model will be accepted as fact, with the caveat that there may be things we cannot yet see or do not yet know that will cause us to modify the five-force model in the future.

In contrast with inductive reasoning, deductive reasoning establishes conclusions with certainty. Conclusions can be certain in situations that satisfy two conditions. The first condition for deductive legitimacy is that specific formal relationships—like membership, correlation or causation—must hold among premises and conclusion. The second condition for a deductive argument to establish a conclusion with certainty is that the premises and conclusion must be both falsifiable and true. We will discuss these conditions further in the next section.

For now, let us conclude this section by noting that arguments may contain both inductive and deductive elements. For instance, an argument with a deductive form overall may have premises supported by inductive reasoning. Distinguishing between induction and deduction is an important part of critical reasoning because it enables proper evaluation of the evidence used to support premises and conclusions.

Modeling Relationships to Build Strong Deductive Arguments

Having identified the conclusion and determined whether the argument is inductive or deductive in form, it is now time to identify the statements or premises that offer the best support for the conclusion. Identifying premises is like assembling a jigsaw puzzle. The picture on the cover of the puzzle box is the conclusion, but we must look inside the box and find the pieces that fit together to create a copy of the cover picture. In a well-reasoned argument, the premises must both fit together properly and contain information that provides meaningful support for the conclusion, just as the pieces of a puzzle must both fit together and add part of the content that makes up the cover picture.

To consider whether premises fit together properly, it is useful to label the elements of each premise with labels or tokens that help illuminate logical relationships like membership, causation or correlation. In Figure 1 above, the premises establish membership relations that establish the truth of the conclusion with certainty. The argument in Figure 1 uses deductive reasoning. The first premise asserts that all fish are animals with gills. We can illuminate the logical claim made by this premise by substituting the letter 'A' for 'all fish', and substituting the letter 'B' for 'animals with gills.' Premise 1 then reduces to the logical assertion 'All members of set A are members of set B.' Similarly, we can depict Premise 2 with the logical assertion 'All members of set C (trout) are also members of set A (fish).' It follows, therefore, that, as long as these premises are both falsifiable and true, all members of set C (trout) must also be members of set B (animals with gills).

Situations where there is strong evidence of causation may also favor the deductive form of reasoning. If I turn the key in my ignition, that will cause the engine of my car to start. I can depict this relationship with the shorthand expression 'IF A, THEN B.' IF I can affirm the condition 'A' (turning the key in the ignition), THEN the condition 'B' (car engine starting) must follow. See Figure 2 below.

If-Then Premises Express Causation or Strong Correlation

Premise 1: If I turn the key in the ignition, then the car will start.
Premise 2: I turn the key in the ignition
Conclusion: The car will start.

Figure 2

But wait! You may correctly assert that there is something missing in the last paragraph. The logical relationship between turning the key in my car's ignition and the starter beginning its activation of the engine depends on the assumption that the car is in proper working condition. This assumption is implied but not stated. We call such assumptions implicit premises. Implicit premises must be true in order for the conclusion to follow from the premises that are stated. We use implied premises to simplify expression of the most critical elements of an argument by omitting obvious or irrelevant conditions. See Figure 3 below.

The examples shown in Figure 2 and Figure 3 are cases where an argument relies on a strong causal or correlation relationship between the 'IF' clause and the 'THEN' clause. Because of the strong relationship between these conditions, when we affirm the antecedent—the 'IF' condition—it is reasonable for us to conclude that the consequent—the 'THEN' condition—must follow.

Implicit Premises, if Obvious/Irrelevant May be Unstated

Premise 1: If I turn the key in the ignition,
AND the car is in working condition, then the car will start.
Premise 2: I turn the key in the ignition
Conclusion: The car will start.

Figure 3

Conditions that are truly related in this fashion allow for a slightly different type of deductive reasoning as well. In cases where a premise of the form 'IF A, THEN B' accurately describes the relationship between conditions A and B, we can use the absence of condition B to conclude that condition A is not present. See Figure 4. This follows logically simply because the IF-THEN relationship means that B is ALWAYS present when

A is present. In a case like this, if B is NOT present, A cannot be present either.

Denying the Consequent Allows Denying the Antecedent

Premise 1: If we drop a raw egg on concrete, then the egg will break.
Premise 2: The egg is NOT broken.
Conclusion: Therefore, we did NOT drop the egg on concrete.

Figure 4

It is important to note at this point that the IF-THEN relationship described in Figure 4 is a one-way relationship: dropping a raw egg on concrete implies that the egg will break, but the fact that a raw egg has broken does NOT imply that the egg was dropped on concrete. Something else could have caused the egg to break. Someone could have struck the egg with a hammer, or cracked it into a bowl while preparing a recipe. The point here is that, while denying the consequent as shown in Figure 4 does logically imply the denial of the antecedent, affirming the consequent has no logical force. The fact that an egg is broken does not logically force us to conclude that it was dropped on concrete. There are many other possibilities. On the other hand, the fact that a raw egg is dropped on concrete does logically imply that the dropped egg will break; therefore, if we know the egg is NOT broken, we know it was NOT dropped on concrete.

There are, of course, situations that exist in the world that are best modeled as two-way IF-THEN relationships. In these cases, we need both conditional statements IF A, THEN B and IF B, THEN A to describe the relationship between A and B. Consider the example case where two neighbors happen to belong to the same Fruit of the Month Club. Each month, the club members receive one box of fruit. We can model this situation with two distinct IF-THEN statements. The shorthand for expressing this relationship in one statement is to say A IF AND ONLY IF B, as shown in Figure 5.

An Example of a Two-Way If-Then Premise/Relationship

Premise 1: Jerry and John belong to the same Fruit of the Month Club.
Premise 2: Jerry gets a Fruit Box IF AND ONLY IF John gets a Fruit Box.
••••••••••••••••••••••••••••••

Premise 3a: Jerry gets a Fruit Box.
Conclusion a: John will get a Fruit Box.
••••••••••••••••••••••••••••••

Premise 3b: John gets a Fruit Box.
Conclusion b: Jerry will get a Fruit Box.

Figure 5

Another type of premise useful and necessary to model certain relationships is the conjunction, commonly known as the 'OR' statement. There are two distinct types of conjunction relationships: the EXCLUSIVE OR and the INCLUSIVE OR. These two types have distinct logical characteristics. We consider each in turn.

The EXCLUSIVE 'OR' is used to model a series of conditions of which only one can exist at any given time. Logically, we say the conditions in the EXCLUSIVE 'OR' are mutually exclusive. This type of statement might

An Example of an Exclusive 'OR' Premise in An Argument

Premise 1: The light switch is in the 'on' position OR the light switch is in the 'off' position.
••••••••••••••••••••••••••••••

Premise 2a: The light switch IS NOT in the 'on' position.
Conclusion a: The light switch IS in the 'off' position.
••••••••••••••••••••••••••••••

Premise 2b: The light switch IS in the 'on' position.
Conclusion b: The light switch IS NOT in the 'off' position.

Figure 6

describe a situation such as whether the light switch in a room is in the 'on' position or in the 'off' position. See Figure 6. In the EXCLUSIVE 'OR', the negation of either side of the 'OR' statement implies the affirmation of the other side. Likewise, the affirmation of either side implies the negation of the opposite side.

The INCLUSIVE 'OR' statement describes conditions where EITHER OR BOTH (or ALL) sides of the conjunction may logically coexist. Because the INCLUSIVE 'OR' describes situations where all of the conjunctions can coexist at the same time, the INCLUSIVE 'OR' premise is not as powerful in eliminating possibilities and arriving at a conclusion. The simple example shown below illustrates the logical characteristics of the INCLUSIVE 'OR' statement.

The INCLUSIVE OR: For Cases Where Either *or Both* Sides of the Conjunction Can Coexist

Premise 1:Either the door is open OR the window is open (OR BOTH)
****

Premise 2a: The door is NOT open.
Conclusion: The window is open.
****

Premise 2b: The door IS open.
Conclusion: The window may be OPEN or NOT OPEN
NOTE THAT BOTH THE DOOR AND THE WINDOW CAN BE OPEN AT THE SAME TIME. PREMISE 2b DOES NOT ALLOW FOR NEGATING THE OTHER SIDE AS IN FIGURE 6.

Figure 7

Note that Premise 2a above works the same way as Premise 2a in Figure 6. For both the INCLUSIVE 'OR' and the EXCLUSIVE 'OR', at least one side of the conjunction must be affirmed. Therefore, if we negate one side of the conjunction, the other side must, logically, be affirmed. On the other hand, Premise 2b in Figure 7 does not work the same way as Premise 2b in Figure 6. That is because, in the INCLUSIVE 'OR', it is logically possible (but not necessary) for BOTH sides of the conjunction to be affirmed at the same time. Therefore, affirming one side of the conjunction neither affirms nor negates the other side of the conjunction.

Summary

Critical reasoning is the process of offering evidence in support of conclusions. Depending on the conclusion one is trying to support, and the type of evidence available, the process of reasoning may be inductive or deductive or both. Inductive reasoning is the basis for the scientific method, and always allows for epistemic uncertainty. Properly formulated deductive arguments can establish conclusions with certainty. In all types of reasoning, it is important that premises accurately model conditions and relationships in the world. Facts, perceptions and values may inform the premises we use to support our conclusions. Arguments are more or less reasonable to the extent we can agree that the premises meet the standards for truth (correspondence, coherence, falsifiability), and the relationships between premises and conclusions accurately reflect the world we experience. We may acknowledge an argument is reasonable even if we do not agree with its conclusion, presumably because we find another argument *more* reasonable.

Chapter I: Overture

1. What are the five most important national political problems facing the United States today? *Solution is based on student/teacher discretion.*

2. For one of the five problems you identified complete the following analysis: (a) Why is this problem so important? (b) Does the problem involve a conflict of constitutional principles? Which constitutional principles are in conflict? (c) List the values that support each side of the conflict. (d) How do you think the conflict should be resolved? *Solution is based on student/teacher discretion.*

3. In Essay 1, the author states that he began his blogging project with the belief that that Constitution was built around mutually consistent principles. Based on this belief, the author thought that increasing understanding of these consistent principles would enable compromise. Using the principles of critical reasoning identified in Appendix 1, one way we might describe the author's original argument as follows:

Premise 1: If the Constitution consists of mutually consistent principles, then ensuring full understanding of the principles will enable political compromise.

Premise 2: The Constitution consists of mutually consistent principles.

Conclusion: Ensuring understanding of these principles will enable compromise.

Why does the author now believe this original argument was flawed?

The author points out that experience teaches us that understanding of constitutional principles, by itself, is not enough to enable compromise. In essence, experience teaches us to deny the consequent of Premise 1 (see Appendix 1). If we must deny the consequent, then the antecedent to Premise 1 must also be denied. This reasoning leads the author to realize that constitutional principles can be mutually consistent, but they are not necessarily so. Sometimes, people's values make them unwilling to compromise on the principles they believe should take priority in a particular situation.

4. In Essay 1, the author concludes that the master virtues of our republic should be humility, tolerance in pursuit of truth, and compromise. What reasons does the author use to support this conclusion? Can you organize the author's thoughts into an argument supporting his conclusion?

Premise 1: IF we are to achieve the purposes enumerated in the preamble to the Constitution, THEN we must be able to peacefully agree on the application of constitutional principles in every case.

Premise 2 (implicit): The social contract for Americans commits us to achieving the purposes enumerated in the preamble to the Constitution.

Conclusion 1: We must be able to peacefully agree on the application of constitutional principles in every case.

Premise 3: IF we must be able to peacefully agree on the application of constitutional principles in every case, THEN EITHER there is only one right application of the principles on which we can agree OR we must compromise on our individual definitions of right application of principles to achieve agreement.

Conclusion 2: EITHER there is only one right application of the principles on which we can agree OR we must compromise on our individual definitions of right application of principles to achieve agreement.

Premise 4: There is NOT only one right application of constitutional principles on which we can agree.

Conclusion 3: We must compromise on our individual definitions of right application of principles to achieve agreement.

Premise 5: IF we must compromise on our individual definitions of right application of principles to achieve agreement, THEN we must practice humility and tolerance.

Conclusion 4: We must apply humility and tolerance.

Chapter II: Start With Humility

1. What is the thesis of Essay 5? What reasons does the author give to support this thesis?

Thesis: The constitutional scope of the government of the United States includes the power to take reasonable measures to ensure a level economic playing field.

Reason: The ability to spend one's time as one sees fit is freedom (aka liberty).

Reason: Freedom is directly affected by how much money a person has.

Reason: Random circumstances of birth dramatically constrain how much money the average person has.

Reason: A system whereby one person's freedom is dramatically constrained due to random factors is less just than a system in which random factors are minimized to some reasonable extent.

Reason: According to the Constitution, the purposes of the United States government include establishing justice and securing liberty.

Reason: If the purposes of the United States government include establishing justice and securing liberty, then the scope of the government's authority includes reasonable steps to mitigate random factors that constrain economic achievement.

2. Do you agree or disagree with the thesis of Essay 5? Why or why not? *Solution is based on student / teacher discretion.*

3. Essay 6 refers to the "argument from disparate impact." Write out the premises and conclusion that you think the author means when citing the "argument from disparate impact."

Premise 1: Part of the Civil Rights Act of 1964 states that a system, policy or practice that creates a pattern of results among people of different race, ethnicity or other protected class different from that group's share of the population has a disparate impact on that group.

Premise 2: Any system, policy or practice with a negative disparate impact on a protected class that cannot be justified on the basis of business necessity is a violation of the Civil Rights Act.

Premise 3: Some system, policy or practice is shown to have a negative disparate impact not justifiable under business necessity.

Conclusion: That system is discriminatory as defined in the Civil Rights Act.

4. The United States Constitution identifies six purposes for the American government (see Essay 5). Pick two of the six purposes and describe a situation in which these two purposes conflict with one another. Discuss

how you think the conflict should be resolved.
Solution is based on student / teacher discretion.

5. Do you think political contributions should be considered constitutionally protected free speech? Why or why not?   *Solution is based on student / teacher discretion.*

Chapter III: Fix Yourself First

1. We all have bias. Discuss an area where you believe your confirmation bias may interfere with your ability to accept or evaluate information. What steps can you take to mitigate your bias?
Solution is based on student / teacher discretion.

2. Does the Constitution of the United States contain mechanisms that help us mitigate the confirmation bias of individual political leaders as we make national decisions? Why or why not?
Yes. The system of checks and balances prescribed in the Constitution establish multiple procedures for the consideration of dissenting viewpoints and collective decision-making. These protections offer ways to mitigate our natural individual bias by enabling the open, collective consideration of diverse sets of facts and opinions.

3. Identify at least four sources of national and international news. Discuss why you feel these sources are (a) reputable, and (b) provide adequate coverage of the spectrum of opinion.
Solution is based on student / teacher discretion.

4. What is the thesis of Essay 10? What reasons does the author give to support this thesis? Write out the reasons and the thesis in the form of an argument (premises and conclusion).
Premise 1: IF confirmation bias teaches us that our individual beliefs and values are not as accurate as we believe them to be, THEN we should be appropriately humble when evaluating the merits of our individual beliefs and values versus the merits of others' beliefs and values.
Premise 2: Confirmation bias teaches us that our individual beliefs and values are not as accurate as we believe them to be.

Conclusion: We should be appropriately humble when evaluating the merits of our individual beliefs and values versus the merits of others' beliefs and values.

5. Essay 12 describes the plot of an episode of Star Trek. What is the moral of this episode? Construct a deductive argument with this moral as its conclusion.

We must set aside hatred and prejudice in order to work together and solve our most difficult problems.

Premise 1: Hatred and prejudice can warp our accurate perception of reality.

Premise 2: We can solve difficult problems when we see the reality of those problems accurately (implicit).

Premise 3: If hate and prejudice can warp our accurate perception of reality, then we must set aside hatred and prejudice in order to work together and solve our most difficult problems.

Conclusion: We must set aside hatred and prejudice in order to work together and solve our most difficult problems.

6. In Essay 13, the author argues that systemic racism and sexism still exist in American society today (2021). Write out the author's argument for this conclusion. Can you identify any premises that are themselves the conclusions of arguments that rely on inductive reasoning?

Premise 1: *IF there is a pattern of disparate impact in the distribution of social goods like wealth, health, and protection of civil rights along lines of race and gender, then there is systemic racism and sexism in American society today.*

Premise 2: *There is a pattern of disparate impact in the distribution of social goods like wealth, health, and protection of civil rights along lines of race and gender in America today. (conclusion of separate inductive argument)*

Conclusion: *There is systemic racism and sexism in American society today.*

Chapter IV: Facts and Fake News

1. Explain the line of reasoning Descartes uses to prove knowledge is possible. Write the premises and conclusion in the form of a deductive argument.

Descartes' argument relies on conceptual knowledge, which often serves as the foundation for deductive reasoning. In short, he claims that the very concept of thinking requires that the thinker exist. Therefore, even though some all-powerful being could deceive him by making the content of his thought an illusion, he still could be certain of his own existence as the thinker.

Premise 1 (implicit): The concept of "thinking" means that a thinker exists and has one or more thoughts.

(alternatively) I am thinking IF AND ONLY IF I exist and I have one or more thoughts.

Premise 2: I am thinking.

_____

Conclusion: Therefore, I exist.

2. Essay 20 defines how a proposition may be shown to be true by coherence. Write out a deductive argument that you think best represents the author's reasoning in this essay.

Premise 1 IF proposition, "A", along with all its necessary antecedents and consequents, does not generate a contradiction when combined with the set of all other true propositions, THEN proposition "A" is true by coherence.

Premise 2: Some proposition, "A", along with all its necessary antecedents and consequents, does not generate a contradiction when combined with the set of all other true propositions.

_____

Conclusion: Proposition "A" is true by coherence.

3. Are there different kinds of facts? Describe and discuss how the three conditions of "knowing" discussed in this section apply to historical facts, scientific facts, and demographic facts.

Yes, there are different kinds of facts, and the differences between types of facts lend make different kinds of reasoning more suitable for supporting each type. Some examples of different types of facts include historical facts, scientific facts, and demographic facts. All facts can satisfy the conditions of knowledge—justified true belief—by correspondence, coherence and falsifia-

bility. For instance, the fact that Pompeii was destroyed by a volcanic eruption in 79A.D. can be confirmed by correspondence with factual physical evidence: we can visit the site of Pompeii, study the deposits of ash and the victims of the eruption, and determine the truth of the facts in that way. We might also study contemporary narratives of what happened from the perspective of other observers, and we might compare the consequences of other volcanic eruptions to our observations of Pompeii. In this way, even if there was less direct evidence of Pompeii's fate still in existence, we might be able to use coherence with what we know about volcanic eruptions in general, as well as the state of technology in the time of Pompeii, to establish the truth of our assertions about Pompeii. Finally, although it is difficult to imagine given the weight of the evidence we have about Pompeii, we can certainly imagine a set of theoretical / hypothetical discoveries that might cause us to question the current narrative of how Pompeii was destroyed. Imagine, for instance, that we discovered that the Carthaginians had developed a super weapon capable of destroying a city by causing an explosion similar to a volcanic eruption, and we discovered a message from the Carthaginians to the Romans threatening to destroy Pompeii, and we found a series of narratives from other civilizations indicating Pompeii was destroyed in an act of war. We might consider these to be falsifiability conditions for our current historical narrative. We could reason in a similar way about scientific facts, with one major difference. With scientific facts, it is usually the case that we can construct experiments in the present and predict the outcomes of those experiments as ways to confirm that the falsifiability conditions for a given scientific fact are not met. Also, with scientific facts as well as with demographic facts, we often find ourselves dealing with statistical evidence. Such evidence may be more suitable for arguments that rely on inductive reasoning as opposed to deductive reasoning. It is also possible, of course, to combine inductive and deductive reasoning in a single argument.

4. Essay 21 makes an argument that both the choice to believe in a religious intuition as well as the choice to not believe in a religious intuition are both reasonable choices. Write out a deductive argument that you think best represents the author's reasoning in this essay.

Premise 1 IF the set of all facts can neither refute nor establish whether religious intuition is true, THEN both the choice to believe one's religious intu-

ition on the basis of faith as well as the choice to disbelieve all religion on the basis of fact are reasonable choices.

Premise 2: The set of all facts can neither refute nor establish whether religious intuition is true.

Conclusion: Both the choice to believe one's religious intuition on the basis of faith as well as the choice to disbelieve all religion on the basis of fact are reasonable choices.

5. Explain how Ockham's Razor supports falsifiability as a criterion for truth.

Ockham's Razor is the idea that, when comparing theories, the one that relies on the fewest assumptions is generally the best. This supports the idea of falsifiability, which is the idea that, in order to be TRUE, any proposition must have a set of conditions that would clearly prove it NOT TRUE. If there were no constraints on making assumptions, then any theory that was disproved by its falsifiability conditions could simply be supported with an assumption that negates one or more of the falsifiability conditions. Consider the ancient Ptolemaic view that the earth was the center of the universe. There were extremely complex models that were built on the Ptolemaic concept, but Copernicus' theory that earth was just another planet orbiting around our sun was simpler and more powerful. One can imagine, however, for every observation that favored the Copernican model over the Ptolemaic model, one could simply add an assumption to the Ptolemaic system that made it "work" with the new observation. By noting that such ad hoc assumptions are weaknesses for any theory, Ockham's Razor supports the use of falsifiability conditions and observation to support the strongest theory.

Chapter V: Challenges

1. Has technology changed the knowledge, skills and attributes needed for effective citizenship in the American republic? Why or why not?

Student answers to this question may differ. Instructor's should grade responses based on how well they are supported, not based on the simple distinction between yes and no.

Yes. Technology has increased the speed and complexity of individual citizens' interactions with each other and with our government. Technology has dram-

atically increased the "information surface area" for most citizens. In order to practice effective citizenship, we must effectively manage our relationships with each other and with our government and with the overwhelming volume of information which confronts us every day. The knowledge, skills and attributes needed to manage these things are all very different from those needed to be an effective citizen 50 years ago.

2. Has technology changed the authority needed by the government to fulfill the purposes enumerated in the Constitution? Why or why not?

Student answers to this question may differ. Instructor's should grade responses based on how well they are supported, not based on the simple distinction between yes and no.

Yes. Technology has increased the speed and complexity of individual citizens' interactions with each other and with our government. Since several of the purposes of government enumerated in the Constitution require some involvement with these types of interactions, it is reasonable to assert that technology has increased the authority needed by government. For example, government did not need to monitor social media 50 years ago. But now, given some of the threats to our society that have emerged, it is certainly reasonable and necessary for the government to monitor some types of social media posts in order to "insure domestic Tranquility" and provide protection and justice for the welfare of all Americans.

3. Using deductive form, write out an argument that captures the case made in Essay 28 in support of using systems to expand informed access and participation in political processes by all citizens.

Premise 1 IF the quality of election results improves when more registered voters participate, and the number of registered voters who actually choose to participate in an election depends on factors such as whether districts are reasonably balanced, whether voters have enough time to balance voting and their work / family, and whether there is easy access to reasonable, unbiased official information, THEN the country should invest in systems and programs to promote fair districts, adequate time to vote, and access to unbiased official information.

Premise 2: The quality of election results improves when more registered voters participate. (IMPLICIT)

Premise 3: The number of registered voters who actually choose to participate in an election depends on factors such as whether districts are reasonably balanced, whether voters have enough time balance voting and their work / family, and whether there is easy access to reasonable, unbiased official information,

---

Conclusion: The country should invest in systems and programs to promote fair districts, adequate time to vote, and access to unbiased official information.

4. In Essay 30, there is an inductive argument supporting the conclusion that America has a corruption problem in public politics. Write out the premises and conclusion of this inductive argument. Can you also put the argument in deductive form? How?

Inductive Form

Premise 1: While serving as governor of Illinois (after several terms as an Illinois congressman), Rod Blagojevich (D) was caught on tape trying to sell his choice to fill a vacant Senate seat. He was convicted and sent to prison in 2012.

Premise 2: While serving as chairman of one of the most powerful committees in the US Congress, and after 36 years serving in Congress, Dan Rostenkowski (D) was convicted of fraud and sentenced to jail in 1996.

Premise 3: Bob McDonnell (R), former Member of Virginia's House of Delegates and former Virginia Attorney General and former Governor of Virginia, was indicted ten days after leaving office in 2014. He was convicted a few months later of accepting improper gifts and loans while in office.

Premise 4: The longest serving Republican Speaker of the House of Representatives was a child molester before beginning his decades-long career in Congress, and he was convicted of financial crimes and sent to jail a few years after leaving Congress. He is the highest-ranking elected official to serve time in prison as of 2020.

Conclusion: Many examples of criminal behavior relating to corruption and financial crimes among high-ranking government officials shows there is a problem with corruption in the American government.

Deductive Form

Premise 1: IF there are many examples of high-ranking American government officials convicted and sent to prison for corruption and financial crimes, THEN there is a problem with corruption in American government.

Premise 2: There are many examples of high-ranking American government officials convicted and sent to prison for corruption and financial crimes. [Evidence for this is based on inductive reasoning from the examples provided previously.]

Conclusion: There is a problem with corruption in the American government.

5. How are congressional districts determined? What is meant by the statement, "We should not allow politicians to pick their voters"? Do you agree or disagree with this statement?

The United States government conducts a census every ten years to determine the distribution of the population. The 435 available congressional districts are reallocated among the states based on shifts in the population density among the states. Within the states, legislatures or other bodies established by the legislatures draw up the districts, which are then approved by the state legislature. If one party controls the state legislature, they can rig the process of designing districts to dilute the minority party vote and ensure that the maximum number of districts favor the majority party. This is what is meant by "allowing politicians to choose their voters." There is much less accountability when politicians choose their voters rather than voters choosing their elected officials.

Chapter VI: Conclusions

1. What is the author's argument explaining our human tendency for conflict given our overwhelmingly similar biological makeup?

Premise 1: IF the enormous biological similarity between human beings includes mechanisms for forming individual perceptions and beliefs, as well as mechanisms for fearing and reacting aggressively to those who are different than ourselves, THEN our biological similarity may be a cause of human conflict.

Premise 2: The enormous biological similarity between human beings includes mechanisms for forming individual perceptions and beliefs, as well as mechanisms for fearing and reacting aggressively to those who are different than ourselves.

Conclusion: Our biological similarity may be a cause of human conflict.

2. Is biological similarity necessary or sufficient for peaceful coexistence? Why or why not?

No. Biological similarity has nothing to do with peaceful coexistence. Members of many species fight over resources like food, water, mating partners, etc. However, the author points out that it is odd for humans to use our relatively minor (from a genetic standpoint) differences as the rationalization for so much of human conflict.

3. How have cognitive mechanisms like availability and anchoring contributed to the survival of the human species?

Cognitive processes that employ heuristics like availability or the anchoring effect can speed up an individual's response to their environment. Over time, we might expect natural selection to favor members of a species who react more rapidly to their environment.

4. How do the imperfections inherent in our individual perceptions support an argument for social virtues of humility and tolerance?

Premise 1: IF our individual perceptions of a phenomenon are not the complete and accurate set of attributes of that phenomenon, and it is possible to acknowledge the limitations of our individual perceptions through humility, and it is possible to optimize our response to the phenomenon by having the tolerance to combine our perceptions with those who have different perceptions, THEN showing humility and tolerance may help optimize our individual and collective response to that particular phenomenon.

Premise 2: Our individual perceptions of a phenomenon are not the complete and accurate set of attributes of that phenomenon.

Premise 3: It is possible to acknowledge the limitations of our individual perceptions through humility.

Premise 4: It is possible to optimize our response to the phenomenon by having the tolerance to combine our perceptions with those who have different perceptions

---

Conclusion: Showing humility and tolerance may help optimize our individual and collective response to that particular phenomenon.

WORKS CITED

Accountability Citizenship, by Stephen Tryon, United States, XLibris, 2013.

apnews.com, apnews.com/article/barr-no-widespread-election-fraud-b1f1488796c9a98c4b1a9061a6c7f49d, accessed June 20, 2021.

Aristotle, *Nicomachean Ethics*, Martin Ostwald, trans., New York, Macmillan Publishing Company, 1962.

A Theory of Justice, by John Rawls, Cambridge, Massachusetts, Harvard University Press, 1971.

ballotpedia.org, "Disparate impact", ballotpedia.org/Disparate impact, accessed July 25, 2020.

Bowen, Catherine Drinker, *Miracle at Philadelphia--The Story of the Constitutional Convention May to September 1787*; Little, Brown and Company, New York, 1966.

brittanica.com, "Confirmation Bias" by Bettina J. Casad, brittanica.com/science/confirmation-bias, accessed May 8, 2018.

Bronowski, Jacob, *The Ascent of Man*, Episode 5: "Music of the Spheres", London, BBC, 1973.

Brown v. Board of Education, history.com/brown-v-board-of-education-of-topeka, accessed July 25, 2020.

"Close Encounters of the Third Kind", Steven Spielberg dir., Perf. Richard Dreyfuss, 1977, EMI, Columbia Pictures,

Coates, Ta-Nehisi, *We Were Eight Years in Power*, New York, One World Publishing, 2018.

"Dennis Hastert sentenced...", Mike Tobin, April 27, 2016, foxnews.com/politics/dennis-hastert-sentenced-to-15-months-in-prison, accessed April 27, 2016.

Descartes, *The Philosophical Writings of Descartes Volume I*, John Cottingham et. al. transl., New York, Cambridge University Press, 1985.

Diamond, Jared, *Guns, Germs and Steel—The Fates of Human Societies*, New York, W.W. Norton, 1997.

dni.gov, https://dni.gov/files/documents/ICA_2017_01.pdf "Intelligence Community Assessment: Assessing Russian Activities and Intentions i Recent US Elections", accessed January 7, 2017.

Eberhardt, Jennifer L., Ph.D., *Biased Uncovering the Hidden Prejudice That Shapes What We See, Think, and Do*, United States, Penguin Random House, 2019.

Edsall, Thomas B., "What if all politics is national?", September 29, 2015, https://www.nytimes.com/2015/09/30/opinion/what-if-all-politics-is-national.html, accessed Feb 1, 2021.

"Election Security Rumor Vs. Reality", https://www.cisa.gov/rumorcontrol, accessed June 20, 2021.

"...Federal judge eviscerates Trump lawsuit", https://www.politico.com/news/2020/11/21/federal-judge-tosses-trump-suit-over-pennsylvania-election-results-439010, accessed June 20, 2021.

"Feds... allege Johnson illegally donated to Mike Lee...", Tom Harvey and Robert Gehrke, June 20, 2015, https://archive.sltrib.com/article.php?id=2645318&itype=CMSID, accessed July 31, 2015.

Fitzpatrick, John C., ed., *The Writings of George Washington*, (U.S.Government Printing Office, Washington, D.C., 1939), 29:410.

"*Forbidden Planet*" Fred M. Wilcox dir., Perfs. Leslie Nielsen, Walter Pidgeon, 1956.

Franklin, quoted in "Madison Debates September 17", avalon.law.yale.edu, accessed February 21, 2019.

"Gerrymandering", by Christopher Ingraham, washingtonpost.com/news/wonk/wp/2015/03/01/this-is-the-best-explanation-of-gerrymandering-you-will-ever-see, accessed Feb 1, 2021.

Geisel, Theodore Seuss, *The Sneetches and Other Stories*, New York, Penguin Random House LLC, 1961.

google.com, dictionary; 'faith', https://www.google.com/search?q=faith&oq=faith, accessed January 15, 2019.

Griggs, Griggs v. Duke Power Co, casebriefs.com/blog/law/constitutional-law-keyed-to-brest/race-and-the-equal-protection-clause/griggs-v-duke-power-co/, accessed July 25, 2020.

Guthrie, W,K.C., *The Greek Philosophers From Thales to Aristotle*, New York, Harper & Rowe Publishers, 1975.

Isaacson, Walter; *Einstein: His Life and Universe*; New York, Simon and Schuster, 2008.

justice.gov/archives/sco/file/1373816/download "Report on the Investigation into Russian Interference in the 2016 Presidential Election" Volume I, accessed March 31, 2019.

Kahneman, Daniel; *Thinking, Fast and Slow*; New York; Farrar, Strauss, and Giroux; 2013.

Kant, Immanuel, *Critique of Pure Reason*, Norman Kemp Smith trans., New York, St Martin's Press, 1965.

Kessler, et. al., washingtonpost.com/politics/2021/01/24/trumps-false-or-misleading-claims-total-30573-over-four-years/, accessed June 20, 2021.

Mueller, Robert S III, *Report On The Investigation Into Russian Interference In The 2016 Presidential Election Volume I*, Washington, D.C., March 2019.

McCutcheon, "McCutcheon, et. al. v. FEC", fec.gov/legal-resources/court-cases/mccutcheon-et-al-v-fec/, accessed September 24, 2021.

"...McDonnell found guilty...", Rebecca Kaplan, September 4, 2014, cbsnews.com/news/former-gov-bob-mcdonnell-found-guilty-in-corruption-trial/, accessed July 31, 2015.

NAP or National Academies Press, *The Polygraph and Lie Detection*. United States, National Academies Press., 2003.

"Our dna...", Lydia Ramsey Pflanzer and Samantha Lee, April 3, 2018, businessinsider.com/comparing-genetic-similarity-between-humans-and-other-things-2016-5?amp, accessed June 10, 2018.

Pariser, Eli, *The Filter Bubble: How the New Personalized Web is Changing What We Read and How We Think*, New York, Penguin Group, Inc., 2011.

Plato, *Apology*, 32: c-e, in Edith Hamilton and Huntington Cairns (eds.), *Plato: The Collected Dialogues*, p. 18.

Plato, *Crito*, 49-54, in Edith Hamilton and Huntington Cairns (eds.), *Plato: The Collected Dialogues*, pp. 34-39.

Plato, *Republic*, 368-369 and 514-520, in Edith Hamilton and Huntington Cairns (eds.), *Plato: The Collected Dialogues*, pp. 614-15 and pp. 747-751.

psychologytoday.com, "Cognitive Bias is the Loose Screw in Critical Thinking" by Robert Evans Wilson Jr., May 17, 2021, accessed May 17, 2021.

Rattle, Allison, and Alex Woolf, *501 Things You Should Have Learned About Philosophy*, New York, Metro Books, 2013.

"Rostenkowski sentenced to prison," Bryan Sierra, April 9, 1996, upi.com/Archives/1996/04/09/Rostenkowski-sentenced-to-prison/3326829022400/, accessed July 31, 2015.

Sowell, Thomas, *A Conflict of Visions*, William Morrow and Company, New York, NY, 1987.

Sparks, Jared, ed., *The Writings of Benjamin Franklin*, Tappan, Whittemore and Mason, Boston, 1840.

Star Trek, "Day of the Dove", youtube.com/watch?v=T18X_NPnliY, Gene Roddenberry, Perf, William Shatner, 1968.

"The Constitution of the United States", in House Document 112-129, *The Constitution of the United States with Index and The Declaration of Independence*, 25th Edition, 2012.

The Legal Dictionary, "polygraph", legal-dictionary.thefreedictionary.com/Polygraph accessed May 1, 2018.

"The Matrix", Lana Wachowski and Lilly Wachowski dirs., Perf. Keanu Reeves, 1999.

"Trump begs Georgia secretary of state to overturn election results...", nbcnews.com/news/amp/ncna1252692, accessed June 20, 2021.

"Trump commutes sentence...", Adam Edelman and Dareh Gregorian, February 18, 2020, nbcnews.com/news/amp/ncna881051, accessed February 18, 2020.

"Trump Passed Polygraph", *The National Enquirer*, United States, AMI, May 7, 2018.

Tyson, Neil DeGrasse, *Astrophysics for People in a Hurry*, New York, NY, W.W. Norton & Company, 2017.

CPSIA information can be obtained
at www.ICGtesting.com
Printed in the USA
BVHW050935291121
622777BV00017B/771

9 781734 304701